Like A Man In A Raincoat

for Zettha,
May your stars
fall together
in perfect circles
and all your troubles
be worthwhile.

Billy S.
1-10-12

Also by William Gammill:

Dancing In The Quantum
The Gathering
Prune
With Reason, Without Rhyme
The Perfect Poem
The Sometime Place (forthcoming)

Like A Man In A Raincoat

William Gammill

Paradigm Books
A Division of Metamorphosis Group

Like A Man In A Raincoat

Published by Paradigm Books
Boulder, Colorado

www.paradigmbooks.biz

If you are unable to order this book from your local bookseller, you may order directly from the publisher above or by visiting William Gammill's website:

www.williamgammill.com

Cover design by Mule Productions
Cover photo by S. J. Farrand

Printed in the United States of America

Library of Congress Catalog Card Number:

ISBN: 0-9720151-4-0
ISBN: 978-0-9720151-4-1

This book is dedicated to Mule Anne, Possum Child, and The Sweet Pea

Table of Contents

*In the beginning was the Word and the Word was God.
Everything after that is just rhetoric.*

from The Big Book of Prune

Preface
{^}

I am writing this from the end of a rope! You've got to understand that.

And while this would seem to be several stories about different people, it is all one story, one person done like a door, again and again. It is a story triggered by an event several years ago in which I appeared to be abducted by some other-world intelligence, 'alien visitors' if you will, though they no longer seem alien to me, nor are they visitors — some have been here as long as we have been here, perhaps longer.

But this is not a story about alien contact. It is about human consciousness and transformation. The event of my abduction however, real or imagined, not only put its mark on my future but reshaped my past as well, causing me to remember and rethink things that have been happening to me all my life, even into early childhood; things I have managed to overlook, ignore, or deny for so long that they have simply been forgotten. This is an attempt to revisit and perhaps reframe some of those earlier experiences.

This is a book of confessions, true stories about real events involving real people. It is also a book of dreams, visions, out-of-body encounters and otherworld visitations — experiences that have both informed and baffled me throughout my life. Truth is, I cannot remember a time when I was not under the influence of some alien force, call them angels, demons, spirits, extraterrestrials, all 'alien' in consciousness and way outside the human range. There were even times when I felt like I'd been abandoned to earth, my spirit imprisoned in the body of an earth boy. My own grandmother was an alien.

But I don't believe these things are unique to me. I just happen to remember them, whereas most people do not. Fortunately, I have met enough people whose experiences are similar in kind, if not in detail, that I have been able to compare notes and information. And that has led me to believe that the world most people believe to be singular and absolute, is but one in a cluster of parallel worlds arranged like the layers of an onion. And though we have been programmed to perceive only one world, we still have the capability of entering into those other realms which are every bit as real, unique, absolute and engaging as the one in which we live our daily lives. Indeed, they are indistinguishable from our daily lives. (When these things started happening to me, I was just a boy growing up in clichéd circumstances — a kid doing kid stuff in small town America.)

There are many ways to describe the events that follow, from alien abduction, to the channeling of other dimensions, to the expression of multiple selves through a single entity, a single soul. Indeed, the soul itself may be more diverse than previously imagined. I don't know. What I do know is that the human psyche is infinitely more complex than our rational mind would have us believe; and the stories depicted here embody a number of diverse goings on in my soul's heart and mind.

Nor does it matter how you think of these small histories and their collective story; consider them to be the ranting of a personality in crisis and disarray, or as the celebration of a variegated soul, it's your call; like a man in a raincoat, I am simply exposing my innermost self in hopes of a little something in exchange. But be assured, every word is written in the faith that I can trust my deepest instincts. I was made to tell this story. It is etched into my body as well as my brain. Indeed, my body, my relationship with others, my entire personal life has undergone drastic changes in order to accommodate this telling. And it has cost me dearly in the loss of friends and family. I have spent most of my adult life wrestling with angels for the right words to describe what takes place here.

Though I have no grasp of the math, the theory behind quantum physics has fired my imagination and propelled me along for over thirty years. It is within the quantum that I find explanations for passing through walls and bending the limits of space and time. Throw in super-string theories and multiple dimensions, wormholes and time-warp tunnels, and you have all you need to grow a fantastic but perfectly plausible universe. Indeed, if quantum shows us anything it is that everything is made of light; nothing is solid. And inside everything are gateways to an inverse cosmos.

Add to that, a growing belief circulated around the globe of a race of 'star people,' come here to assist planet Earth in her transition into a new age of consciousness — indeed, they may have been here for eons just waiting for this moment in cosmic history. (In truth, they have probably been here through several such moments, playing midwife to the birth of a new human.)

And that brings us to Prune. I'd be remiss if I didn't at least warn you about Prune. This is, after all, as much his story as it is mine. ·

Perhaps the most genuine and unlikely character you will meet on these pages is Prune. He is neither a composite nor an invention. In fact, Prune has been with me since childhood, embodying my earliest memories. Something of a quasi-mystic guide or harbinger of change, Prune claims to have come here from deep in interstellar space, on a mission. (He is also a thief and a liar, but that's a whole other can of noodles.) The amazing thing, most uncanny, is Prune's ability to turn into anything at any time, whether he wants to or not, just by thinking of it — very tricky, and wrought with hazards.

And he seems to have been on planet Earth forever; so long, in fact, he can't always remember why he came here in the first place. Under the human influence for so many lifetimes he has developed a brain-cloud causing his consciousness to blink on and off like a neon sign with an electrical short. Fortunately, as a harbinger he is not required to do much more than *show up* looking as good as someone several thousand years old could possibly look.

Now whether or not you buy into any of this is not my concern. But it helps me — it may not help you at all — but it helps me to better understand Prune's intrusion into my life. I might be wrong. We might all be wrong. The truth might be so outlandish as to be beyond our ability to even imagine it. One thing I do know is that Prune continues to be the most *real* and *alive* thing I have ever known on any plane of existence. The night he disappeared, I was sure I was going to die. Did, in fact. It was the longest night of my life, the most terrible and perplexing and sweet.

*

Before the Beginning
{^}

I can't be sure who died in what order but it was Donnie came to me first, just to say goodbye. Belle followed shortly after, said she needed my help. At first I thought I was dead, and that's why they were coming to me. But I was too miserable for that. Everything I'd heard, led me to believe that dying was easier than this. I was soaked in blood and chilled to the bone.

Someone I knew but did not at the moment recognize, leaned over and drove a stake into my knee. Then he drove a nail into my forehead — the second because the first made me suffer but would not let me die. It was an act of compassion, he reasoned. I was born to die this way. He was just carrying out the edict. That was his role. It wasn't anyone's fault, it just happened that way.

All this, in a strange room, surrounded by people I didn't know. There was a table, a toilet, a bed. I was in the bed and the covers were pulled up under my chin. Someone was trying to wash my face with a dirty cloth dipped in a basin of filthy water. Then my dead grandmother came in and put her hands over the basin and the waters became illumined with a soft interior glow, and for one brief moment I remembered where I was: on a metal cot in a jail cell somewhere in the Sonora Desert. What I thought was blood, was my own sweat. But the pain was real, and all over. I wondered if I might die from it.

Then that same someone I didn't recognize earlier told me he was going to let me die a little. Don't be afraid, he said. It'll be all right. It will help you forget this moment even as you are remembering all the others. And as he said it, I felt the fear and the rage melt away and be replaced by an immense relief that grew deeper as my consciousness trickled away. I felt weightless and pure.

Then I collapsed, shaken by such real death throes that I could not repress the urgency to cry out. This was in Tucson, Arizona. I was in jail, caught with my hand in the pocket of a man recently dead when the police drove up.

*

From The Beginning
{^}

Memory is like a weasel in some regards, wild and unpredictable, aware of everything at once but visible only in darts and flashes. However, a weasel sleeps with its tail draped across its nose, alert and aware of exactly where it begins and where it leaves off. Not so with memory. Memory has no boundaries and no rules and seems to never sleep. How then, to tell a thing like this? It is probably best to start at the beginning and proceed somewhat chronologically. So:

Once upon a time I was a baby. Then, after awhile I became a plumber. And after that a poet. But before that, at about the age of five or six, I was expelled from Bible School and held out of kindergarten for conduct unbecoming — unbecoming *what*, was never made clear, but it probably had to do with unexplained absences on my part; that, and the lies I was accused of telling when I tried to explain that I had been spirited away to some foreign planet on a bizarre craft manned by I didn't know what. But even that was not the beginning.

It all started the night I was born.

My father was downstairs in the pool hall, drinking and playing dominoes with the attending physician, my uncle — who was also the sheriff and my namesake — and a fourth person whom no one could later identify. Sometime after midnight my mother, wearing only a gauze nightgown, began to flip and flop like a fish caught in a net, proclaiming my arrival in a fit of prophecy, any minute, any hour. By the time I arrived it was almost daylight and the domino players had been drinking all night. We were told, *wait a minute! wait a minute! we're almost finished with this hand.* So my mother and I went on alone.

The doctor, drunk and unable to find his instruments, arrived in time to declare that I was a girl, which I certainly am not, then passed out cold. So the fourth person bit the cord in two with his teeth and "took care of it. " No one thought a thing about it at the time. In fact, not until the next day did anyone think to question who the other person was or how he'd come to be there. We were playing partners and needed a fourth, said my father. Whoever he was, he seemed to lose every hand all night and still walked away with everybody's money.

Of course, I don't remember any of that.

But that's what I've been told. And retold. My mother insisted that the mysterious other person was an angel. My father wondered if it could have been my grandmother, who was something of a local legend, an icon of religious folklore known to manifest from out of nowhere on occasions. She died before I was born, but I grew up hearing about her.

The sheriff, my dad's brother, claimed not to know about angels. Nor did he agree with my dad; he just could not imagine my grandmother ever wearing a beard, and he thought she'd given up cigars even before she began evangelizing. On the other hand, no one else remembered the stranger smoking cigars *or* wearing a beard. My Aunt Polly was the only witness that night who was sober and in her right mind, and she wasn't saying anything. An amazing night, she said afterwards, but refused to elaborate.

*

My earliest memory is one of lying in this sort of baby-cage pushed up against the window. Looking up at the brightest thing in the night sky, Venus or Sirius, I suppose, I just *knew* with all certainty *that* was home. That's where I came from. I cried at night if I couldn't see it. No one knew why I cried. I think they thought I had colic, and of course I wasn't old enough to tell them otherwise.

About that same time I became aware of beings coming right through the walls at night and touching me on the forehead. I didn't know what that was all about, but it was a precursor of things to come.

I remember as a very small child being able to think but not speak. And no one around me knowing what I thought, or that I was even capable of it. Images flashed through my head. In one, this giant mother-thing with beautiful blue eyes leaned over and kissed me on the forehead. Then she rocked me a little. It was amazing how much I loved her, this mother. But another part of me didn't even recognize her, didn't feel anything but the calm that attends a soul on its journey. I was aware of that, you know, of myself as a soul. At the same time, I was also aware that I wasn't supposed to be seeing myself as a soul. I was a child living above a pool hall in a small town in the northwest corner of Arkansas. My soul contract had placed me here with good people who loved each other, however briefly.

At the age of three I had an imaginary playmate but had no name for him until I was twelve or thirteen. By then he was too real to be imagined. That would be Prune, of course. About the same time I was coming to life over a pool hall in Siloam Springs, he was getting himself incarnated into the Boston Mountains north of there, just down from Mount Gayler at a place called Shaeburg (a town, incidentally, which no longer exists; in fact, it had pretty much been abandoned by the time Prune arrived.) Prior to that, Prune had been hanging out in an altered state, watching over things from the astral plane, biding his time, picking his place of reentry. "Ahh, I'm back! " he said. "I know how all this stuff works" — meaning the universe at large. Supposedly he recognized his mother and a lot of his friends and family from the 'other' side. But it was frustrating for the first few months, being able to see his spiritual family but unable to communicate with them in any meaningful way. He flailed his arms and legs around, excited when someone he'd known for centuries came into the room. Of course when they saw his waving they thought he was just *so* cute. "Cute's ass," he said, in a language unspoken on this planet for millennia, maybe ever. It didn't take him long to realize that living with your own past mistakes is difficult enough, but also knowing that your true nature is that of an infinite being, makes living here almost unbearable. He pitied the human condition and was grateful not to be permanently bound to it.

For what it's worth, Prune wasn't sure who (or *what*) his father was, but his mother was an unnatural woman, known throughout the mountains as the Angel of Shaeburg Hollow. It was said that by just walking down the street she could make women crazy and impossible to live with, and married men confused about their gender. (More on her later.)

By the time I was five or six years old, I was trying to tell my mother about Venus and the Moon and star people visiting me at night. She listened, and then told me not to talk about such things in front of people. Best to leave it alone, she said. I couldn't very well leave it alone, but I did stop talking about it. Still, I wondered how much she knew that she wasn't telling — and *how* she knew it.

Soon after that my dad left home. Soon after that he came back. He bought us a new house and we all moved in together. Soon after that he left again, this time for good, kind of.

It's like this: my grandparents on both sides were ministers and evangelists, but my dad taught me about the world. He was a good man, a big man, a generous man, I'm told, a man who believed that anything worth doing was worth overdoing. He cut a wide swath, and probably the best thing he could have done for me was to leave when he did, allowing me free rein to grow up and become anything I wanted without having to duck around his shadow — if indeed, he cast one. He would disappear for two or three years at a time and it was as though he had tunneled into another life without telling anyone, including himself. When he reappeared it was usually with a new wife, a new family. I have no idea how many brothers and sisters I have; at last count there were eight of us, but huge chunks of his life were never accounted for. I imagined him, vigorous, unconcerned, in a wilder place, leaving us behind with some notion of respectability while he had already reinvented himself in another part of the universe, just down the road, perhaps, in another county, another state, some city to which I longed to go — not just to find him, but in search of the same thing he was in search of. Growing up, I wanted to take every train that stopped in our town.

And if there really are multiple universes, my father could be living in any number of them still. But in this particular incarnation all he seemed to want was just to drink a little, smoke a little, have a few laughs, and *be* somebody — a sort of low rent Frank Sinatra. Only this Frank Sinatra looked like Clark Gable. I have some wonderful memories of my father, mostly invented, but true nonetheless.

So we sold the house and my mother and I moved into a little apartment on South Maple, with a ravine and a real live vine-infested jungle at the edge of the backyard. Across the street was this pretty little girl-thing whose father owned the Five & Dime Store. I remember once when we were playing ball and jacks, watching her get sucked up from the floor of her living room towards the ceiling. She hung there for a while, suspended by I don't know what, then was returned to the floor where we were sitting together. I looked at her for a response but she just looked puzzled and a little frightened. She said nothing about what had happened. I started to ask her about it, but just then her mother came back into the room, and before long we were playing again. She eventually taught me how to kiss, sort of, but nothing else, and I regret that

Not long after that, and living in this same neighborhood, I met my two best friends, childhood friends of the kind you never get over.

*

The First Time
{^}

The first time I saw Jimmy he was standing on the porch, peeing into the flower bed, watching two blue jays circle and dive at a yellow tabby skulking across the yard. One of the jays flew too close to Jimmy's head and he stumbled backward, pissing on himself and the front door. He said something that a six-year old should not say, twanged his penis one more time, and went inside.

It was a party. We were there to celebrate someone's birthday. I don't remember who.

As the guests arrived they gathered in the living room — short men without beards, men in first grade, bankers, lawyers, bed-wetters, a tough crowd. The birthday party was a thinly disguised cover for what was really going on. We were there to learn about war and practice on one another.

Hands in our pockets, we stood around, jostling, jockeying for place, small fights breaking out and calming down. We eyed each other, cleared our throats a lot, and frowned. Jimmy was standing on a chair beside a table that held the biggest chocolate cake in the world. He had the face of an intelligent six-year old and the body of a well-developed four-year old. He was short. And he never got over it. He had a knife in his hand. He was ready to cut the cake. This wasn't his party, this wasn't his cake, and it wasn't his knife, but he was ready.

Someone questioned someone else's right to be there. *How old are you? I'm seven. Okay.* A seven-year old threatened to beat up a six-year old and Jimmy jumped in and offered to beat them both up.

Donnie was there too, slender and dark, my first impression was that of a raccoon: curious, dexterous, dark-eyed and dangerously charming. He was all boy, wild with mischief but without a mean bone in his body. He was being quiet, watching everything, a look of foolish innocence on his face. We both fell to watching Jimmy, who was leaning on the world the way a sergeant leans on a new recruit. In his most intelligent six-year old voice, Jimmy said, *we could easily kill a three-year old.* And the other men agreed. Even Donnie agreed, but I could see the look on his face, I could tell what he was thinking. *Yes, we could. But why would we* want *to?* Donnie was complex. He was seven years old, but already beginning to think like an eight or nine year old.

By now we were all relaxed and ready to get down to playing war. Everyone pulled their weapon and started ducking behind the furniture. Someone had a cardboard sword. Someone else had a four-barreled pistol. I had a cast iron German Luger (vintage WWII). Someone's mother had taken the knife away from Jimmy but he was still brandishing a Daisy air gun. There was an entire box of weapons to choose from, but Donnie made his hand into a fist, pointed one finger, cocked his thumb and said, *bang*! He was standing in the middle of the room, sighting down his thumb and picking things off. He eyed a pillar in the dining room, pivoted and fired — a hit, you could tell by the flames and smoke reflected in his eyes. When Donnie turned around I jumped out from behind the couch and shot him with my Luger. I could see it burn all the way through him. He clutched his stomach, doubled up in agony and sank to the floor. Dead. He stayed dead for about a minute then jumped up, instantly reincarnated as someone else. I shot him again, and this time he stumbled up the staircase a few steps then fell down the stairs, over and over, clutching his chest, dying and dying.

Donnie continued to die again and again all afternoon. He was good at it. Jimmy thought it was because Donnie was using his hand and not a real (toy) gun. He died willingly and without argument each time I shot him, but seemed invincible to everyone else. Jimmy thought that was because I was using a German Luger — the weapon of choice for my generation.

Probably for that reason, plus the fact that I seemed to be getting a lot of attention, someone convinced Jimmy that he should jump my ass. Never one to need a lot of convincing, he did. I was six, almost seven, but had never been in a real fight before. Not so, with Jimmy.

His first swing caught me dead on the ear. There was an explosion inside my head, then a continuous sound of static, like a radio between channels. It lasted for days. When he swung again I turned away and took his fist on the back of my head. He threw punches from everywhere and all at once. One of them knocked me to my knees. Then he kicked me in the stomach. The kick didn't really hurt but I was stunned by the fact that he had kicked me at all. His commitment was absolute.

Screaming and wailing, I managed to get in a few licks of my own. If anything my own blows were even more vicious than his because I was terrified. I thought he intended to kill me. I stuck my thumb in his eye and bit him on the ear. Two adults tried to separate us but Jimmy rushed me again, arms flailing, fists flying in all directions. He almost knocked me down again but I surprised us both by landing one flush on his nose. He stopped. He looked cross-eyed at his nose. Then he looked at me. "Jees," he said, "whadya hafta do that for?" And it was over. Just like that.

Every other kid in the room was quiet, wide-eyed, behind an adult or flat against the wall, whining for their mothers or to go home. Everyone that is, except Donnie. He was just watching us, grinning, eating a piece of chocolate cake.

And that's how the three of us met. Except for the occasional glitch that comes from mirroring one another's adolescence, for the next ten years we were inseparable.

Of course Jimmy tried me on a few more times, just to make certain the first one wasn't a fluke. He always went insane when he fought, swinging wildly, like a windmill. He had short arms, short legs, small hands; but he had a broad back and thick chest. Occasionally one of his punches would connect and it was devastating. My only hope was to go insane with him. After a few of those, it was decided that we were better off working together. My dad was gone, Jimmy was living with his grandparents, Donnie's own father had died of cancer a few years earlier. We had more to gain by taking care of each other. So it became the three of us against all comers — four, actually, if you count Prune, who had not yet introduced himself but was never far away. My guess is, he was there somewhere but in disguise. By then he was already experimenting with different personality costumes and learning to play hopscotch by jumping from one dimension of reality to another. And not long after that, he was discovered in his neighbor's cow shed, unconscious and lying in a stall where he'd apparently been sleeping the night before, disguised as a milk cow, when he was suddenly and without ceremony milked and raped by an automatic milking machine. In those days Prune still thought of himself as mortal — he had the virtue of doubt, fully capable of making mistakes.

*

By the time we were nine years old, Donnie and I were dreaming each other — visiting each other in dreams. We'd probably been doing it for years without realizing. With a few exceptions, nothing of significance ever seemed to happen in the dreams. There wasn't even much of an exchange between us, just a sort of recognition. I saw him and he saw me, and the next day we laughed about it. It seemed normal enough, but we both knew it wasn't something we could easily share with anyone else. If Jimmy was a part of all that it didn't register, and he certainly didn't have the same recall that Donnie and I had. We didn't know what it meant, if anything, and it seemed to occur less frequently and we talked less and less about it as we got older. In fact, not until the night he died did there seem to be any real purpose for it.

One of those exceptions, however, has revisited me for most of my life. This dream is like a room I measure each time I am in it, and each time I leave I forget its dimensions. It seems to take place in Persia during the reign of Alexander. We are all in costume, warriors in Alexander's army, perhaps generals. The three of us, Jimmy, Donnie and myself are lifelong friends and have been in the service of Alexander for ten years. Donnie and I are having an argument in the dream. I'm not sure what about, but it seems that I have decided to make some dramatic alteration in my life having to do with Persia and the nature of my spirit. Indeed, I am so overwhelmed by my experience in Persia that I have vowed to stop being Greek and become partly Persian. I'm convinced that Donnie needs to make a similar change, but he doesn't see the point. In a fit of rage, I put a lance through him, murdering one of my two best friends in front of the other, and in front of a thousand of our own soldiers. This part of the dream ends right here.

But there's more.

In this other part, I seem to be some sort of 'angel of death,' executioner of God's creatures. I'm concerned they'll think I'm their enemy when I have to strangle them, but God assures me that will not be the case, saying that he'll turn their attention away from me and toward the diseases and the woundings and all the ways they have to die. I'm not convinced but I do it anyway. These words come immediately to mind: *Disease can be cured, a cold can be remedied, but death is by decree.* It seems that Donnie's death has been decreed — the only means of moving him out of one body of consciousness and into another. I am simply the instrument. I still don't want to, but I do it anyway. And in my heart I know it's right. More importantly, I know that Donnie knows it too. He knows it before I do. And knows it better. Nevertheless, I was always relieved to see him in school the next day.

In another dream, we are not the same being, but we seem to share a common soul. I am waiting for Donnie to arrive by train, and when he steps down, not knowing where he is or why he has come, he recognizes me and gives me his hand, lets me take charge of everything that will follow. I open a car door and we get in and drive toward open country, open sky, the two of us searching the heavens for something we know is there but cannot quite remember. As night comes on we see a huge ball of lightening off in the distance and hear grass whispering beside the road, and when stars bear down like music we each begin to understand what we are here for and why things are the way they are between us. And it's all right.

*

Here and There
{^}

At the end of summer, my first day in third grade, we were each asked to stand and tell the class our name and what we wanted to be when we grew up. I knew I was in trouble because I'd had three names in two years and there was no word for what I wanted to be.

"A saint, " I said, after some deliberation. Saint Billy Mack, I thought. It had a nice ring.

But it earned me a lecture on the nature of reality, one with which I took vocal issue, citing my deceased grandmother as an example of sainthood in our family. I'd have been all right if I had left it at that, but I also challenged the teacher's ability to think and walk upright. And that caused me to get sent home for being a heathen and a blasphemer.

Now I had no idea what a blasphemer was, but a heathen is what my aunt called the neighbors when they stayed up all night, drinking, being loud, and probably doing sex stuff to each other. I was confused by the accusation, but not entirely displeased.

21

I was living with my aunt and uncle at the time. My aunt was a lovely, gentle lady who thought she was being spiritual when she berated herself for her sins — not to mention what she could do to me for mine. She was determined that I become a missionary. She read to me from my grandmother's Bible, and taught me about demons and Catholics, that they were both wicked and given to nameless desires.

In Sunday school my aunt taught us that we, all of us, are made from dirt and God spit. And my aunt was nothing if not convincing. When she told me about Eve tempting Adam with an apple, it actually felt like a cold but thrilling betrayal. She made me believe that Noah might well have drowned in the flood, Job might have suffered until he died, and the Ark of the Covenant was our only guarantee against future annihilation —'not by flood, but by fire next time. 'All that. And she made God sound like a petulant old man.

My aunt was a fundamental Christian who believed we were all destined to spend eternity somewhere, heaven or hell, but she suffered from a short attention span. About two years was all any particular sect or denomination could keep her occupied. She went from being a Methodist to a First Christian to a Baptist, back to being a Methodist, then to something Pentecostal, and finally became a Seventh Day Adventist, you get the picture. The theme of her religious persuasion may have altered from time to time, but never her devotion, never her staunch belief that whatever religion she was courting at the time was absolutely the only one that could save us all from perdition.

One night she went for a walk as a Methodist and stumbled into an evangelical tent revival by mistake. The Reverend Pratt called down the wrath of God on all sinners that night. He also called down the love, which sounded exactly like the wrath, on those same sinners. He made fire burn in the aisles and brimstone rain from the rafters; sulfur swirled in the air as the evangelist spit forth a place filled with pitchforks and devils and lakes of fire that burned forever. God made a place like that because he loves us so much, said the Reverend Pratt. Then he performed healing miracles and addressed the fate of the damned — he was an expert on demons and the dangers of becoming possessed. Very impressive. My aunt said he looked like Tyrone Power, give or take a few pounds. A lot of women found the Lord that week.

Finding the Lord was one thing, keeping Him was another. My aunt figured the best way was to keep the Lord's emissary close at hand, so she invited the Reverend Pratt to stay over for the remaining days of his crusade in our town. Our house was small, just room enough for my aunt and uncle and cousin. I slept on the couch unless we had company, in which case I 'vacationed' with another aunt and uncle on the other side of town.

I came back two weeks later and the good Reverend was gone, but there was a picture of my aunt flanked by the Reverend on one side and my uncle on the other. My uncle seemed to be the only one in the picture actually enjoying himself. My aunt kept the picture by her bed, said it helped her with her visions. She actually had dreams and visions not unlike those of William Blake, the visionary poet and painter. Only she had never heard of William Blake, and couldn't tell the kingdom from the outhouse. And she couldn't paint.

The image my aunt had of me was what she hoped I'd be, built around a reality that was strictly her own. My image of myself was all wrapped up in things that were...well, foreign, to say the least, probably otherworldly, and certainly nothing my aunt understood or cared to hear about. For instance, one cold night in January I wasn't feeling well so I went to bed early, but was unable to sleep. I lay there, eyes wide open, thinking about everything and nothing, awake and stuck. Suddenly, I felt a hard thump from some unseen source and began floating up and away from my body — my body, as I knew it anyway. And when I was again able to stand, I was on a desert with hot sands under my feet. I looked around and seemed to be on a dune or ridge of some sort. The frightening part was how real the whole thing felt. It was exactly as if I'd been snatched out of bed and transported light years away to another planet deep in space, and abandoned there. Except that *there* was actually *here*. A mood of desolation swept over me as I realized that I had been taken an impossible distance from home, abandoned by my parents, and cut off from any recognizable lifeline.

I sat bolt upright in bed, feeling the coldness of a winter night in Siloam Springs. For one terror stricken minute I couldn't figure out if I was there or here.

The next morning I tried talking to my aunt about what had happened, but she didn't want to hear it, told me I scared her when I talked like that. So I stopped trying.

From that point on there were differences between us that I was not allowed to talk about or acknowledge. I started hiding things from her, from my mother, everyone. I got so good at hiding stuff that I eventually succeeded in hiding it from myself.

Religion was a dream I was born to — unfinished business, I guess. I bought into the whole sanctimony of it: the doctrine, the dogma, the angst; by the time I was eight years old I was a regular pre-pubic Savanarola, convinced that our church was God's Elect. I was too young to realize this as a stance common to the human species — each one thinks it's God's only. But the more I was made to hide things, the less sure I was, and the more suspicious I became.

Unaware of my suspicions, my aunt believed that I could do very little wrong. And when I got sent home from school for the 'saint' thing, she forgave me, and admitted that any ill feeling she might have toward saints was because they tended to all be Catholics.

*

Not long after that I had a seizure in the middle of a Wednesday night prayer meeting.

But before I tell you about that, I should tell you about Sister Bull.

Sister Bull was an inspiration to our church, a true saint if ever there was one. She spoke in tongues on occasion, but mostly she interpreted for others. It works like this: as the Spirit moves through, someone, anyone in the congregation, might begin to speak in some foreign tongue or language unknown to the rest of us, unknown to the Devil, indeed, unspoken on the planet. In a most unearthly way, it is a strange, almost syllabic but consistently repetitive sound. Not only is it impossible to ascertain it's meaning, you can't even recognize the words being spoken, if words they are. And that's where Sister Bull came in. She could turn all that gobbledygook into real words and sentences. Her interpretation didn't really explain anything, but it did so in correct English.

I liked Sister Bull. I liked her a lot. But sometimes she scared me; like the time I saw a yellow ring of light around her head and remarked about it out loud and in the middle of church services, wouldn't stop talking until my aunt threatened me, made me promise never to mention it again.

Three nights later I had the first of a series of seizures. It was a cold night, a week or so after Christmas, following the altar call. I was kneeling beside a dozen other sinners, each of us praying for the same thing, I guess, to be forgiven, and then entered by the Lord. I was eight years old and very good at imitating behavior I thought to be adult and somehow correct. But at some point I lay down on the floor in front of the altar and got very quiet. Not normal. Noise was normal. Shouting, moaning, beseeching the Lord at the top of one's voice was normal. Quiet was aberrant behavior.

Suddenly everyone got quiet with me, even Sister Bull. Everyone was listening to me be quiet. Then I began to talk in a very low and distinct manner about things to which I had no clues.

I was assumed to be in a state of rapture, rare, but not unheard of in our church. Of course I don't remember much between the time I responded to the altar call and opening my eyes an hour later, staring up into this sea of tearful, smiling faces. What happened in between depends on who is telling the story. The Lord works in mysterious ways, said my aunt, and led me up the aisle, out the door, and into the crisp night air where my uncle and someone were waiting for us, warming up the car.

Who's that, I said, pointing into the backseat.

I don't know, said my uncle. I thought he was with you. In the backseat sat Prune, disguised as the littlest general in the world; he couldn't have been over three feet tall. He was wearing a tunic with gold buttons and a hat with gold braid and a star. He had a silly grin on his face and looked as puzzled as I was about how he got there.

Make him go away, I whined. Then I began to cry.

I was shivering and mumbling, and my aunt hugged me close to her all the way home. It would be the last meaningful hug I would get for a very long time.

That Sunday the pastor told everyone how full of it I was, the Spirit, I mean. He talked about me for ten minutes and I pretended to read the Bible the whole time. I was embarrassed, and afraid of being found out.

For the next few weeks I tried to make myself as normal as possible. But word got around. I was suspected of rapture, and no one knew quite what to do with me. It was decided that no one should put his hands on me in any casual or offhand way. I don't know who decided that, or if it was just a given. All I know is that I was eight years old and suddenly no one; not my mother, not my aunts, my uncles, no one would touch me. Not long after that, I began having seizures in odd and inconvenient places. And not long after that, I began touching myself, but there was nothing casual or offhand about it.

And reality continued to be a big concern of mine — I was convinced there was only one. My job, as I saw it, was to track reality down by exposing the falsehoods superimposed on it, and replace them with my own.

*

Dumb Bear
{^}

I was in the hospital recovering from something no one was able to identify or put a label on. According to the doctor, I was not sick and had no symptoms, but I might be terminal. More than that, he couldn't say. It was enough to put my aunt in a panic and cause my mother to insist that I tell her why I hadn't spoken a word since the afternoon of the eclipse.

I couldn't talk. Or *wouldn't* talk. Hadn't said a word for days or weeks — no one could quite recall. Except my mother. She blamed it on the eclipse.

I was nine years old and had been talking since I was two, reading since I was four. Then, one day I just quit, talking that is. In an effort to see what other skills I might have lost besides that of speech — you know, in case I'd suddenly become stupid as well as mute — the nurse asked me to describe my neighborhood, specifically our next door neighbors. It was a trick question and I knew it. We had no neighbors next door; there wasn't even a house, just an empty field. And besides, I wasn't talking, remember?

Still, I wanted to tell her something. I mean, she was old and kind of edgy, but she deserved something for her efforts. I considered telling her about a pair of shameless hussies that occupied the house across the street — actually there were three, if you count the mother. (I debated on how much to tell the nurse, but figured, what the hey, she asked.)

The two hussies were sisters; one, a year older than me, the other, a year younger. Perfect. (I wouldn't know *how* perfect for a few more years.) They lived with their parents who were seldom seen and never around; they didn't even come home some nights. The father was a big, thick, brute of a man who talked through his nose when he talked at all, and carried a loaded gun in a pocket of his overalls. My Aunt Polly said he didn't love his wife or like his kids so he stayed gone all the time. He was a truck driver and a killer, I guess, always on the road. His wife was an alcoholic. And she smoked too much. She smelled like something dying or recently dead. Anyway, the two of them were gone a lot and the girls were left alone, kinda.

It was the older sister who drew everyone's attention, had since she was twelve or eleven. Early in the evening, men would come by and knock on her door — afternoons, too, as soon as she got home from school. Sometimes they lounged on the porch, smoking, chewing tobacco, and spitting — committing all the sins of the world, according to my aunt whose job it was to preserve the sanctity of the neighborhood.

My uncle thought the neighborhood was just fine the way it was. He didn't always agree with my aunt's assessment of how the universe should be run, though he never said as much to her. One afternoon, looking out the window and talking on the phone, he noticed the older sister standing on her doorstep, watching the street. She appeared to be naked. His face flushed and he leaned so far forward he almost fell out of his chair. I saw it too, but before I could yell the alarm my uncle put his finger to his lips. "Shh," he said. "Put a cork in it."

He hung up the phone and seemed to study her person for a long time — soft features, sunk in fatty folds, but muscled too. I guess she had a sexy shape, but I didn't know it at the time. She just looked naked and scary to me. However, my gaze, once it began to hover around her body, just would not return home. (I wasn't sure I wanted to tell the nurse that or not.)

My Aunt Polly believed that if you lusted after something enough, that thing would happen and you would get eaten by it. By the same token, she believed if you prayed for something long enough that too, would happen. My mother thought it was all in the mind — if you thought about something, anything, enough that thing was bound to come to you. I asked my uncle if that wasn't the same thing.

"Yeah, yeah," he said. "Everything is everything." Then he looked at me in a way that made me very uncomfortable. "It's all God, you know."

I had a feeling that my aunt would disagree, but she wasn't there, so it didn't matter.

What did matter was this problem I was having with the nurse. If I had it to do now, I'd tell her about the time, a few years later, when Jimmy and I were at the movies. It was Saturday morning at the Grand Theater. We had dates, sort of. We were sitting with the two hussies and things looked promising. We were on our best behavior. But when Jimmy came back from the restroom he carelessly left his fly undone. As I stood up to let him pass down the aisle, I whispered it to him. Embarrassed, he tried to zip up and sit down in one discreet motion, but the girl sitting in front of us had too much hair hanging across the back of her seat. As Jimmy sat down and zipped up, he caught a snatch of her hair in his zipper causing her head to snap back and a loud stream of invectives to pour out of her mouth. None of us knew quite what was going on. She was draped across the back of her seat, leaning precariously into Jimmy's lap. He couldn't get his fly undone. They were like that for a long time it seemed, her screaming and trying to pull her hair free without losing it, Jimmy, reluctant at this point to unzip his fly for any reason.

In short, Jimmy and I were made to leave the theater. We were incorrigible. We were disgusting. Our mothers should be ashamed of us. All that. The two hussies were quick to say they didn't really know us, that we'd just come in and sat down beside them when the movie started.

Anyway, that's what I'd tell the nurse if I were telling it now. But I was just nine years old; remember? None of this had happened yet. And besides, I wasn't talking to anyone — not my mother, not my father, certainly not the nurse.

I was in the hospital because I wouldn't talk. It was presumed that I *couldn't* talk. Not true. I talked to myself, to my stuffed animals; I talked to beings that no one else could see. In fact, that's where most of my attention was focused, but I'd learned not to talk about that, not to anyone.

So, most of what I had to say was said quietly, privately, or not at all.

I wasn't talking. It was presumed that, since I couldn't talk, I couldn't hear. It was also presumed that since I couldn't talk or hear, I couldn't read. Don't ask me how they made that connection — the world is not a simple place. Anyway, I was left with very little to entertain myself. I read labels on jars,

31

instructions on walls, a pamphlet explaining how to exercise an artificial limb. I tried to build a cave out of mashed potatoes and gravy, but the gravy was too watery. The cave kept falling down, and even when it stood up I didn't have a bear or anything to put in the cave. So I invented a story about a bear who froze to death because he lived on the wrong side of the mountain and couldn't find a cave for the winter, and me with an empty one to spare. That made me even more miserable. Dumb bear, anyway, I said, under my breath, but with the nurse standing right there within earshot.

It was enough to jolt me out of whatever private non-verbal place I was in, and back inside a purely human dimension. Of course the nurse heard me wrong and took it to mean something else, something personal. I think she thought I thought she was a really dirty person.

Meanwhile, not far away but in a world I couldn't begin to imagine, Prune was having his own troubles. He was forced to give up his digs on the outskirts of Shaeburg and move into a cave in the side of a bluff overlooking the town. This, because the town itself had been abandoned and then overrun by wild hogs — not razorbacks or javelina, but domestic pigs gone bad. (I swear I'm not making this up. I spent a night in Shaeburg ten years later and there were feral hogs everywhere; no people, just hogs, left there, I guess, when the railroad shut down the water station and the residents moved out overnight; I was there investigating the very real possibility that I had, at another time in another life, actually grown up in Shaeburg. But that's another story; in fact, it is fast becoming another book.)

And it begs the issue, that when I said 'Dumb Bear,' the nurse thought I was calling her a dirty name. Things got ugly and complicated after that, and eventually led to my hurried release from the hospital. It's like that, you know; you create something, then you get involved. And you never know where anything will lead.

*

A Visit From Grandma
{^}

For decades a story gossiped in my hometown had to do with my maternal grandmother. Revered as a folk-goddess by some, thought to be a witch by others, it was said that she could read the stars, interpret dreams, and heal by the simple laying on of hands — acceptable stuff in our community. She was also rumored to hypnotize, teleport, levitate, and speak in tongues. And that made some people nervous.

More than one account has her appearing outside the door of someone sick or dying, in the middle of the night and without being summoned. She was always alone. She was usually barefoot and wearing a gauze nightgown. She went directly to the person's bedside, said very little, and didn't stay long. Afterwards, no one could recall by what means she had come and gone. And some sort of miraculous healing usually followed.

Of course all that came after her 'conversion.' Which was sudden and total and came in what should have been the middle of her life. I say, 'should have been,' because her life was cut short by a coincidence so miraculous and unbelievable that my mother refused to even talk about it.

Before her sudden change, grandma spent her days working in the tobacco fields and her evenings cooking for grandpa and their six kids. She read the bible, prayed some, and chewed tobacco. Nothing unusual. She was a good woman, said grandpa, even before her conversion. An absolute miracle, he said of her afterwards.

Grandpa came from different stock. He was educated. His own grandparents once owned those same tobacco fields grandma grew up tending. He taught music and math in the local grammar school. And he worshiped grandma. He once told someone, Prune, I think, that not everybody likes what I like. If they did, they'd all be after your grandma.

Then one day, grandma stood up in the middle of the field she was working. She looked up at the heavens and down at her feet. Her six year old daughter, my mother, was following her, whining about something, wanting to be held. She realized that she'd never once kissed her own daughter because her mouth was always full of tobacco. It was a complete realization.

Grandma spit once, huge, walked out of those tobacco fields that day, and never went back. Said she refused to do to others what she would not do to herself.

Like a stone into gold, she changed.

It was like some 'other' being had taken up residence in grandma. Grandpa noticed the other being right off, and liked it so much that he quit his job the very next day in order to follow her around and facilitate her new life. Grandpa became a carpenter and itinerant handyman. Grandma became an evangelist.

Accompanied by grandpa and their six kids, grandma walked all over the Cookson Hills, preaching the spirit of the gospel to any one who would listen. She held tent revivals in places where there were no towns and no roads. They had no house and no car. They had a circus tent and a mule. They had each other. They had the Lord.

And they lived that way for six years. Until she died, and the mule died, the kids all left home, and grandpa went quietly insane.

All this was before I was born. Most of my memories are concocted from family folklore and a photograph of her that sat on my mother's dresser. In the photograph, my grandmother was wearing a sackcloth dress that hung to the tops of her bare feet. She held an open bible in the palm of one hand. She had this really soft, grandmotherly smile on her face. She was not old as grandmothers go, but she had this huge mane of silver-white hair. The way the light filtered through her hair made it look like her whole head was on fire.

I never actually met her, of course. But once, in the middle of the night, during an awful time in my life, I was laying in bed, waiting (I'd been waiting for weeks, listening to doctors talk about me as though I were not in the room, overhearing my aunt tell my uncle that I was too sensitive to live), just waiting, when the door of my room swung slowly open. For a moment the doorway remained empty, then I saw my grandmother's form taking shape in the opening.

"My son," she said, moving toward me and becoming more solid and recognizable with every step. "There are no mistakes. And you are never alone. I live in a world where everything is beautiful and everyone is kind. I know you still believe in a world of punishment after death. And as long as you believe that, then it is true. The world is exactly what you think it is. That much never changes." She told me that I would live a safe life this time. That I could go anywhere, do anything, suffer any consequence. I could live my life on the edge, and know that I was protected. Then she seemed to put one hand on my forehead and another over my heart. After about a minute of this, she reversed the two hands. I felt a tingling in the bones of my soul. After another minute, she turned and moved away, growing more misty and undefined as she approached the door. She left the same way she had come.

Almost immediately after my grandmother left I saw a light above my head. A tube emerged from it and I was sucked upwards, like a speck of dust drawn into a vacuum cleaner. The next several minutes — or hours? — are a blank. The very next thing I remember was being in a flowerbed outside my window at home, except that there is no flowerbed outside my window. There were two tall light beings with me, and a smaller being whom I now know to have been Prune. After being shown several images, which I did not understand and cannot now remember, I was sent back. The nurse entered the room during this experience and thought I was dead, even told my mother as much.

But within hours I was running up and down the corridors in my hospital nightgown. I flashed an old lady, flipped a nurse off, and was on my way home by mid-afternoon.

*

The Last Ballgame
{^}

Jimmy played right field. He didn't necessarily choose right field so much as accept it. His legs were short. He had little bitty hands. He couldn't run fast, couldn't throw far, a .250 hitter. Right field was the one position where he could cause the least damage to the team. Everyone knew that. Jimmy knew that. He didn't like it, but he knew it. And if he overheard anyone talking about it he would bust them in the mouth. Two things he did have going for him: He had broad shoulders; the shoulders of a normal person, maybe bigger even than a normal person. And he had an attitude. Of the group of guys I hung out with, Jimmy was the first to realize that a fist to the face was more effective than any amount of kicking and scratching and calling each other names. Still, he played right field. He was playing right field the day the three of us, Jimmy, Donnie and I played our last ballgame together.

After too many balls went out to right field and never came back we went out to check on him. It was a long walk — he always played deep. We found his ball cap on top of his mitt on top of his shoes. It was a perfect illusion. But Jimmy was gone.

There was no way to tell how long he'd been gone. Had he played almost any other position his presence, or lack of it, would have been noticed. But he was gone and it didn't take long to discover that he had taken my bicycle with him.

He didn't take Donnie's. Donnie's bike was a piece of junk made from the spare parts of 37 other bicycles. Mine was almost new, a Western Flyer with a tank in the middle and a saddle basket on the back. Jimmy took mine because he knew I'd come looking for it. And he knew Donnie would come with me because he always did, and because baseball bored Donnie almost as much as it did me. So we went in search of Jimmy; Donnie on his bike, me on Jimmy's — did I mention about his short little legs?

He wasn't hard to find. We knew where he'd be. He knew that we knew. And he had a plan.

We went straight to Gregory's Newsstand on Broadway. Squeezed in between Nora's Cafe and the Western Auto, the Newsstand was little more than a wide hallway with a glass front. It was lined with magazines and newspapers, and had a pinball machine in the back. My bike was leaning against a parking meter out front. Jimmy was inside abusing the pinball machine. His plan was for the three of us to climb up the new fire escape at school. It was Saturday morning and no one would be around.

The grade school was straight up the hill on Broadway. It was a red brick building with wooden stairs, wooden flooring, wooden everything, four stories high, five, if you counted the basement. Just a week earlier, a tubular fire escape had been added to the outside of the old building. A window on each floor had been altered to accommodate the tube. By exiting through the window you found yourself in a high-speed descent down and around the enclosed tube and launched into mid air at the bottom.

It was Jimmy's idea to climb *up* the inside of the fire escape and slide down. But when Donnie got to the top floor, he accidentally leaned against the window-door of the escape tube and it came open. Suddenly we were inside the building. Once inside, we became other people.

We dumped bookshelves. Moved desks around. Turned trashcans over. No real damage. Until Jimmy wrote a dirty word on the chalkboard. I wasn't even sure what the word meant exactly. They both seemed to know, but argued over its spelling.

The next day my uncle and another policeman came to school and talked to several boys with bad reputations. Nobody thought of us. The reason nobody thought of us was that we were pretty courteous in school. We fought amongst ourselves, and Jimmy had his bluff in on most of the younger boys in school, but we didn't talk back to the teachers, and, in the presence of the older and really tough kids in school, kids who'd been in the sixth grade for two or three years, we were colorless. Of course my uncle being sheriff didn't hurt our cause either.

At the end of the day, Mizz Cruz, the principal, came on the public address system and announced that the guilty parties had been identified. Before taking action, however, these individuals were being given a chance to come forward of their own accord. A voluntary confession would mitigate their situation considerably. It was a bluff and we knew it. We trusted each other. While one of us might confess, we were not likely to implicate the others.

In short, we got away with it.

A week later we came back after a matinee and did it again.

We became bold, cocksure, even arrogant. We waited two weeks and did it again. This time we broke a rotating world globe, stopped up one of the toilets, and scribbled more obscenities on the chalkboards. Jimmy drew a picture on the wall of the girls' lavatory. I didn't understand the picture but it would eventually get us busted.

Right after homeroom period on Monday, Mizz Cruz visited each classroom and demanded the names of those responsible for putting such filth on the walls of our school. There were delinquents in this school. They would probably grow up to be perverts (or Catholics.) They had names, and she wanted those names right now.

Mizz Cruz was soft-spoken but hard-nosed; she meant what she said. I knew she wouldn't let it drop, that she would keep at it until we were caught. I was scared. I couldn't stand the thought of being caught wrong. Even more than her anger, her righteousness scared me to the point where my stomach cramped. I had diarrhea. I vomited — actually the vomiting was a ruse, a visible display of how really sick I was in order to get sent to the nurse's office. But the diarrhea was for real. As the afternoon wore on all my symptoms got worse. I was in the nurse's office, laying on a cot, sweating, facing the wall, when the principal finally came for me.

She touched me gently on the shoulder. Are you through being sick, Mr. Gammill? she said.

I gave her a confused look and said, No ma'am, I'm not.

She grabbed me by one ear and sat me up. Get over it! she said.

I gave her my best rendition of what it looks like to be innocent, wrongly accused, and without comprehension. The nurse came to the doorway and asked what was going on. The principal told her I was faking.

I'm not, I said. I swear I'm not.

He really is in pain, said the nurse. Can't you smell him?

I could smell him halfway down the hall, said the principal. But he's faking it. He's just trying to avoid being punished for his disgusting behavior.

I was crushed. I couldn't bear the thought of anyone thinking I was the kind of person who would write filth on bathroom walls and then shit all over myself to throw them off the track. I couldn't imagine who would do such a thing — well, Prune maybe, but not me. In that moment I was absolutely convinced of my own innocence. I tried to say something along this line, but the principal wasn't buying any of it.

As it turned out, Donnie had already admitted to everything anyway, claiming to have acted alone. But no one believed him. And besides, it was Jimmy's artwork. He had apparently drawn the same thing on a young lady's homework that he'd drawn on the bathroom wall. For all the hubbub, it was determined that Jimmy's drawing was anatomically correct, and no kid his age should know that much about anatomy — it just wasn't natural.

I held out for my innocence, refusing to admit to anything. But since they were both my very good friends, I offered to help in making restitution. And since nothing but human decency had been destroyed, it was decided that restitution would involve one month of working on weekends and after school, whitewashing walls, picking up the school grounds, all that.

A couple of weeks into our penance, a classmate of ours was found floating face down in an abandoned well. That took the heat off of us. The drowning took place on Mrs. Rotrammell's vacant lot, a mine field of goat manure and abandoned wells that we'd all been warned to stay away from. Our classmate and his dog had both drowned. Apparently one had fallen into the well and the other had gone in after him.

Then it was summer. Donnie and I played a little sandlot baseball, but not Jimmy. He went into training. His uncle put up a speed bag and a punching bag in his garage, and Jimmy started training to be a real fighter. Donnie and I were a few years from becoming local phenoms, better than average high school athletes. Jimmy went on to become a Golden Gloves state champion, poster boy for the Arkansas Ring Magazine.

Everything was still to be done, the road rising up in front of us like a ladder. I'd found out some things about myself I didn't want to know. Prune was finding out some things too. He'd temporarily given up his cave and moved away from Shaeburg in order to better understand cause and effect, and what it's like to grow up human in a linear reality — that, on the outside chance he might run into a similar situation elsewhere in the universe.

Barefoot and semi-literate, Prune arrived in Siloam Springs alone and unannounced. It was said that he arrived one day and all the birds left town the next. Never mind that it was the beginning of summer, the birds left anyway. And not long after that, three doctors determined that Prune had an arrested development. He didn't know what that meant exactly, but it made him shy and awkward. He took to hanging out in the alley or on the corner, down the street and under the stairs just fondling his arrested development. The first time he got caught with it showing, he considered hanging himself from the railroad trestle that crossed the creek behind the barn behind the well house. He considered drowning himself in that same creek. Sager Creek, I think it was. The barn and the well house actually belonged to my Aunt Juliet and Uncle Lacey.

It wasn't a serious consideration, however. He figured, what-the-hey, no history is final, and began taking his arrested development out at picnics, parties, PTA meetings (someone's bastard, no doubt). He was moving so fast in so many directions involving different costumes and parallel lifelines, he was bound to make mistakes. Something of a body-ventriloquist, he once projected his body so far he couldn't locate it for three days. And when he did, it was in Amarillo, Texas locked in the men's room of a Sinclair Service Station. I'm just thankful I didn't know him then. No one did, not really. And if they did, they weren't about to admit it.

*

Living With My Dead Aunt
{^}

It was a lucky thing for me my uncle died when he did.

Of course it wasn't lucky for him. And I don't mean to say I was glad to see him go. I liked him. I liked him a lot. But when he died he left my seventy-year-old Aunt Juliet living out in the country by herself. She didn't drive, didn't even own an automobile. And she couldn't hear well enough to talk on the telephone. Aunt Juliet had two sons and a daughter who lived nearby with their own families, but she wasn't about to abandon the only home she'd known for fifty years to go live with a bunch of goddam people she didn't even like that much. Someone had to stay at the house, not really to take care of her; she was fully capable of doing that herself, but to be there in case something unforeseen happened.

I was twelve years old, a townie — I'd never lived on a farm before. It had a cow and a goat, a few chickens. Not much of a farm, but farm enough for me. And I wasn't expected to do much. The farm was Aunt Juliet's job. It was her life, and she didn't want me relieving her of it. My job was to see that she didn't fall down and break something and die before anyone discovered her; that, and keep the gypsies from

45

stealing the eggs from her chickens and the milk from her goat. The cow, a Guernsey named Janet, was sort of a watchcow. She didn't give milk anymore, but she mooed at things in the night. My Uncle Lacey used to take a thermos of coffee to the barn at night; he'd sit and drink coffee and smoke his pipe and talk to Janet till all hours. Now that he was gone, I think she missed him.

Living with my Aunt Juliet was a mixed blessing that took some getting used to.

My parents were off somewhere having their own adventure. For the past year I'd been living a few miles up the road with my Aunt Polly and Uncle Gark and a brat cousin named Karen. The toilet was outside, cold and nasty. I slept on a small couch in the living room that was way too short for my feet and legs. And I had absolutely no privacy, not a corner or a box to call my own.

At Aunt Juliet's I had my own room, my own bathroom (indoors), my own house even. I mean, living with Aunt Juliet was like living with a ghost. She was almost invisible — about a half step behind her deceased husband was my guess. There were times when we would pass in the hall and the look in her eye told me she had no idea who I was or what I was doing there. I might as well have been living alone.

It's not like we were new to each other, suddenly thrown together. When I was small I spent summers with her and my Uncle Lacey. We liked each other a lot. Everybody thought it would be a good fit, no trouble, a good circumstance for both of us. I was at school all day, and continued to take my meals up the road with my aunt and uncle. Aunt Juliet got to stay in her own home surrounded by her own memories, her own stuff.

About the only thing we ever really did together was watch the late news on television. That was on weeknights. And with the sound off. Any time we watched television, it was with the sound off. I'd turn the sound up, and she'd turn it down. I'd turn it up, she'd turn it down. Without gesture, without comment, without acknowledging my presence in the room, she'd turn the sound completely off the instant after I'd turned it up. On Saturday nights we watched Live Wrestling, and Liberace, both with the sound off. I can't tell you how disturbing that was. Still is.

I don't mean to suggest that Aunt Juliet and I had been rudely abandoned to each other. Nothing of the sort. Her daughter took her shopping with her several times a week. Her son took her for long rides in the country. Her grandkids had her over for dinner. But she seemed most at ease when she was in her own home, down in her own storm cellar.

From early April to mid July she seldom left the cellar except to eat, emit, and milk the goat. There was a generator down there, and a radio, a refrigerator, a light and a chair. But most of the time she just sat in the cellar with the lights off, in absolute quiet. I walked in on her once, sitting down there in the dark. I called to her. Nothing, not a word. I was afraid the obvious had happened. I called to her again. Shh! she said. Hear it? The tiny dry sound of a spider pissing?

I don't think they had any idea how far gone she was.

Most of the time she didn't seem to be happy and she didn't seem to be sad, she just seemed to be dead. And since my real reason for being there was to see that she didn't fall down dead and stay dead for too long without being discovered, the whole thing got strange. I got strange. Being twelve years old and living alone in a house with a dead

47

person does things to you, things you don't realize for twenty or thirty years, things you never get over.

Still, I liked the privacy of having my own room. I liked the autonomy, the freedom to come and go at all hours with really no one to answer to. I felt like Tom Sawyer except that my Aunt Polly lived a mile away and had no idea what I was up to most of the time. I was out of her hands. I was out of everyone's hands. No one could have anticipated what was in store, where it would all lead.

It lead right to Grandma Belle's front door.

Grandma Belle lived across the road and two doors down from Aunt Juliet's place. You could see her porch from our porch. You could see her in the yard with her dog.

She was the real prize, the reason behind the reason for my being here, living with my Aunt Juliet. I knew who she was, had known about her all my life — we were almost related. And I'd heard the rumors. But getting to know Grandma Belle intimately over the next few years would prove to be a significant watermark in my life. It would prepare me for everything that came later — namely, Prune.

An untamed miracle, said my Uncle Lacey, of Grandma Belle, just before he died.

That Woman! said Aunt Juliet.

*

Grandma Belle
{^}

That Woman was Grandma Belle.

Grandma Belle lived on the side of a hill overlooking the creek, in a frame house the size and shape of a chicken coop. In fact, it used to be a chicken coop. Her house was set wrong on the property, so you could see the end of her porch, but not the front of the house. With the windows boarded up, and the roof covered with moss, the house looked like a giant bird's nest. Stacks of lumber, used bricks, and garbage littered the yard. There was a small fishpond filled with sand. There was a concrete deer beside the pond, and a plaster flamingo. Pink.

Grandma Belle wasn't really my grandmother. She was my Aunt Polly's mother. And she was part Cherokee. I don't know which part or how much, but Grandma Belle was actually born on a reservation in the Cookson Hills of Oklahoma.

I don't know what her real name was, her Cherokee name. No one had spoken it in so long that it had simply been forgotten. I'm not sure she remembered it. She was older than everyone I knew, and for that reason almost everyone called her Grandma — unless she wasn't being particularly grandmotherly. Then they called her Belle. She called herself Belle.

She called herself Belle because she insisted that her own mother was Belle Starr, the infamous, cigar-smoking lady bandit who once rode with Jesse James. On the other side of the feather, Belle's father was a genuine tribal chieftain. His name was Hammer-Head; at least that's what my uncle called him. Hammer-Head supposedly stumbled over Miss Starr one night while she was camped under a deep cliff-overhang above the Illinois River. The camp sight was marked by a bell with a star inside it, both carved into the limestone cliff face. A deep scar, eroded by water seepage and overgrown with moss, the carving is about the size of a man's hand, and can't be seen by the casual observer. It can't even be found without a guide, someone who's been there. I've been there. Belle took me there. She said it was carved by her mother and marks the very spot where she herself was conceived.

Anyway, there it is, if you know where to look. It's a real place, not far from another real place where, together with my two best friends, I uncovered a shallow grave with the remains of nine skeletons in it, skulls and all. The bones all belong to the University of Arkansas now, but I could show you the hole, maybe even dig up some bone shards. I've taken a number of people there over the years. It's not far from where Belle taught me how to dance one moon-crazed night. And not far from the cave at Lookout Point, the place where my best friend disappeared inside a limestone boulder.

Belle or 'Grandma,' was my first teacher, I guess. Other than the stuff you learn in school, which isn't much. She lived with her husband and Smokey. Smokey was part collie and part shepherd, and looked like a wolf. I don't remember much about Grandma's husband. His name was Ethan and he drank a lot. My uncle said that was because of Belle. Who knows?

Smokey and Grandma waited for me after school, both of them on the porch swing. Every manner of broom, bone and rag seemed to be rotting on the porch. There was an occasional chair without an arm or a leg or a seat. There was a jug missing an ear, and a cat with no tail. A great iron kettle stood at the end of the porch. Huge and immovable, it was large enough to hide in. I don't know where it came from; it had always been there. It rang like a bell when you struck it, and with the tips of your fingers you could feel the black metal sing for a long time afterwards. Sometimes Grandma sat in the kettle, waiting for me. Sometimes she put Smokey in there. I don't know why.

It's hard to describe someone you know so well. Probably the first thing you noticed were her eyes, black, as brilliant as a hawk's. Her thick white hair was held in place by a cap of black netting, though she wore braids as well. And she wore a shawl around her shoulders night and day, all year round. The shawl is worth noting because she was always knitting something new into it; a shawl so phenomenal that people who had never seen it, swore to its existence, even describing it in such detail that it had become a part of the town's collective memory.

She loved cats and dogs and small animals. She brought rats in from the barn and turned them loose in the house. Grandma Belle in a house was more or less like a mermaid in a ship's cabin. She preferred it populated with the very element it was meant to exclude. She had crickets in the pantry, squirrels in the eaves, a bat in the attic. She had this old nasty rooster that abused his wives and generally ran the barnyard his way. He was slim and tall with greasy black feathers and a yellow ruff like a collie dog. He could make the dirty feathers around his neck stand up and fall back down whenever he got mad, just like flexing a muscle. I was sitting on the porch stoop one day shelling peanuts when he attacked me. He thinks you're a chicken, said Grandma Belle. You have to show him you won't put up with any nonsense. She picked up a stick and threatened him with it until he backed off and began pecking in the yard.

A few days later, I walked in and caught her naked in a tub of water with that same old dirty rooster, its feathers caked with mud. It might've died if I hadn't cleaned it up, she said, and laughed, genuinely, without being self-conscious.

I guess Grandma Belle was beautiful as a young woman. When I knew her she just looked scary. Everything sagged and drooped. She had false teeth but kept them in a bowl on a nightstand, beside the Bible. The Bible was always open to a picture of Jesus wearing a dress. Jesus' hair was done up in a Toni, and he was surrounded by a lot of little boys without scars or physical impairments. There were candles and crosses and beads on the table as well. It looked like some sort of shrine.

Pure subterfuge, said my Aunt Polly. Grandma Belle was a heathen at heart. (That, in the words of her own daughter.)

Remember, this was in the heart of America, home to a number of Christian cults embraced by people who are upright, righteous, and largely governed by commandments that begin with, Thou shalt not!

Horseshit, said Grandma Belle to all that.

I guess the shrine was there to throw zealots and nosey neighbors off the track.

I'm not sure what Grandma saw in me. Maybe she thought I was an orphan, which I wasn't. True, my dad lived in

Wichita, and my mother in Tulsa, but I had aunts and uncles and cousins everywhere. I had Jimmy and Donnie. And of course there was Prune and Arlene, but I didn't know that yet. There was Jenny Lynn, but I'd only just found that out and wasn't at all sure what it meant.

Nevertheless, Grandma decided to save me from myself, and started by teaching me things I wouldn't begin to understand for another twenty years; and some things I'll probably never fathom.

She taught me slowly but in spurts. I wouldn't hear from her for a spell and then I couldn't get rid of her. Not that I wanted to be rid of her. But a little of Grandma Belle went a long way. Especially when she was being crazy. Of course, I never thought of her as crazy. But she could tax your sense of decorum at times. And everyone else called her crazy, so it was hard not to join in once in awhile, even if you knew better and didn't really mean it. Her own people said she was 'witco,' meaning, crazy-holy. And she did have some peculiar ways.

Every few months Grandma Belle would steal me away from the house and take me up into the hills a few miles from where we lived, to the place where she grew up. We would set out walking in the late afternoon and walk until it was dark, the moon high in the sky. I'd stumble along behind her through thickets and scrub oak and poison ivy, convinced we were lost. We never took the same route but we always ended up in the same place, a bluff at the edge of a cleared circle in the woods and high above the river. When we got there Grandma simply grunted and told me to sit down.

She would walk around the edges of the clearing doing peculiar things with her hands in the air and mumbling what sounded to me like a prayer but not like any prayer I'd ever

53

heard. At the back of the circle was a huge boulder, maybe ten feet in diameter and almost perfectly round — one of God's marbles, I thought; a shooter. Grandma would say something to the boulder, then she would sit down beside me, and in a quiet, dangerously intimate way, tell me to do something like, think of the worst thought I could, something I'd done, or the most terrible wish or fantasy that I carried around inside myself, some feeling that I suppressed and hoped no one would ever find out. She'd tell me to think of it, bring it to mind *right now*.

I'd be so terrified that I could hardly allow the thought to surface for fear she might see it or hear it or, in some mysterious way, divine it without my saying anything. I was convinced that she could hear the awful content of my mind. She encouraged me to look at how vulnerable I was, how frightened I was of exposing my self. And to *what*?

After a long silence she would say: Now let me hear it. Share this terrible thought you hold in your mind.

I would usually laugh nervously, or cry, or both, even as I shared my darkest secret. And as I brought my secret into the light, she would say something like: See? The world didn't break. Your mind hasn't shattered. My ears didn't fall off. Nothing is the worse for your confession.

And in that moment, though I did not understand much of what she said, I knew what it meant to me: that nothing need be sheltered, denied, or protected; there is room enough in the heart for any of the mind's meanderings.

Afterwards, she would sit on the edge of the bluff overhanging the place in the woods where her village used to be — now under twenty feet of water. She would pull her shawl up around her, light her pipe and smoke, while I took off all my clothes and danced around the clearing, and danced and danced and danced until I was exhausted.

We'd return home in the middle of the night and my Aunt Polly would be furious. She wanted to know where had we been, what were we doing till all hours? Had Grandma behaved herself?

Of course I didn't tell her anything. It was a secret between Grandma and me. I knew that, without being told. In fact, I'm only now beginning to talk about it.

*

All this dancing naked in the woods stuff started when I was about eleven or twelve years old.

I had a history of seizures that looked like fits of temper, ugly to look at and way out of control. One afternoon I was playing with my cousin, and all of a sudden I started carrying on like a crazy person, slamming doors and windows, smashing up all my toys. I threatened to tear my cousin's gizzard out if she ever spoke to me again. She was a year younger than me, and took it to heart. She cried. My aunt cried. For the first time in my life, my uncle cuffed me one behind the ear. It didn't help matters. Nothing did.

Until Grandma Belle appeared out of nowhere. She swooped in the front door trailing her shawl behind her, wrapped my coat around me, took me by the hand and headed off down the railroad tracks, telling my aunt not to worry, we'll be back after awhile, don't wait dinner.

I was stunned into silence.

I followed her down the tracks like a whipped dog.

We followed the tracks for three or four miles then skirted the dam at Lake Francis and headed up into the hills toward the round boulder and the clearing in the woods. We talked as we walked but I didn't hear much of what she said. It was dark by the time we got there.

She wasted no time.

She told me we were there to dance. She told me that her ancestors came here to dance during each full moon. The moon wasn't full but we were going to dance anyway. It was a dance, she said, if done swiftly could not be seen by the human eye. Then she began to circle around me, slowly and deliberately. She pulled her shawl up around her shoulders and hummed to herself.

I did not see her move, but her fingers stroked my nose and suddenly I could smell fresh cut hay from fields as far away as Kansas. I could smell butter melting on toast in my mother's kitchen. I felt a fluttering at my ears, a snap of Grandma's fingers, and I heard a train whistle and a warning bell at the crossing near my Aunt Juliet's house several miles away. I heard someone call my name. A flick of her foot at my genitals and I got a boner and didn't know *what* to do. I was embarrassed. I cried. I began to walk, slowly at first, and in huge circles. Then I began to sing and take my clothes off, spinning around the very edge of the clearing, naked, doing a dance I did not know, had never known, and would not be able to remember or repeat five minutes after it was over.

Meanwhile, Grandma had moved to the edge of the bluff and sat down, her back to me, smoking her pipe, staring into the dark above the lake that covered the village where she was born. This went on for hours.

At one point I became aware of something strangely familiar behind me that I knew would not be there if I turned around suddenly, and would only come closer when I looked away. I sang and danced and cried until something inside me exploded and my body just gave out.

I lay down slowly, loosely, and slept.

And dreamed.

I dreamed a lot, but all I can recall is being naked and high up in the mountains, so high that there were no trees, only wind and landslides and frost, but none of these felt cruel or uncomfortable. Looking down from the mountain, I saw a woman sitting in a bed of flowers trembling in the wind. I had the odd sensation of descending upon her gently like snow.

When I woke up, Grandma had covered me with my clothes and built a fire. It was still dark, cold in the early morning hours. But I felt good. I felt relieved of something; released into something else, something larger and more wide open, something for which I have no name. I could not remember ever having felt better in my life.

Afterwards, Grandma told me that I could go back there and dance anytime I felt ugly or mean or overwhelmed by the booger inside me. She said I didn't actually have to go there in my body; that I could go in my mind. She taught me how to do that. But it would be years before I would remember what she taught me, and put it to use.

She said something else that night, something that sent a chill up my spine and proved to be oddly prophetic. She said, there are magnificent beings on this earth, son, walking around posing as humans. I don't want you to ever forget it.

As if I could.

I am old, she said, and my brain cells are dying, millions of them at a time. Of my earlier lives in Egypt and Atlantis I recall very little. I only mention those places because soon everyone will begin to remember them and talk about them, mostly people who need to feel better about themselves and cannot.

It was the first I'd heard mention of Atlantis but it caused the hair on my neck to stand up. Didn't know why. We were both quiet on the way back, neither of us saying a word, until she remarked, "You know you're being followed, don't you?" And for some reason I told her, yes, I knew that. But I didn't know who, and I didn't know why. I don't know what Belle knew. Something probably.

*

I spent a lot of time at Grandma Belle's, but I can only remember sleeping-over one time. It just happened to be the night her husband, Ethan, died. They always went to bed early and this night was no exception. It wasn't even dark outside.

The strange thing is, I don't remember how I came to be there that night. It certainly wasn't something I looked forward to. As much as I liked Grandma, her house was scary, she was scary. And her husband was a mystery that remains unsolved to this day. He once told me that all he wanted from the afterlife was to be buried in a shallow grave, so he could feel the rain. But mostly I remember him spitting tobacco into a coffee cup and leaving it for someone else to clean up.

It was still light outside when Grandma came into the room with her nightgown on and her teeth out, to tuck me in. She knocked and I lay there stiff as a plank under the blanket. When I didn't say anything she came on in, without her regular clothes on, with her arms and feet exposed, her mouth folded in on itself. "G'night, honey," she lisped, and patted me on the head as she turned out the lamp. And there I was, bored, restless, unable to sleep while the two of them snored so loud it made the windows rattle. I lay there for what seemed like a

long time, then got up and tiptoed all over the bedroom, stared
out the window for awhile watching the sky turn black and the
stars come out. I quietly opened all the drawers of all the
dressers in the room, took some things out, examined them,
put them back. I didn't dare leave my room for fear of running
into something untoward — her husband, the dog, a flock of
bats, whatever specters might be flying around, anything was
possible. I thought about counting sheep but I'd been so
warned against sleeping with sheep that I couldn't concentrate,
couldn't even imagine what one looked like. I knew but I
didn't know, just as I couldn't always conjure up the faces of
my mom and dad. I lay awake for hours, staring out at the
Milky Way, watching the moon rise and sink.

Sometime in the night I must've dozed off because I woke
up with a start. Something was going on in the room. There
were beings of light everywhere, and these ashen beings inside
silver tubes of light, their eyes coated with a kind of
translucent film. They seemed to be moving through an
atmosphere of oil and water that would not coalesce. A band
was drawn tight around my biceps and my fingers tingled like
they were going to sleep. I'm not sure what happened next or
what had gone on before. What I do know is that in that split
nanosecond between sleep and waking, right before I began to
doubt, I felt like I was just moments away from going
somewhere, home maybe.

Grandma's husband didn't get up for breakfast that
morning. He died in the night. I don't know what Grandma
knew or when she knew it, but she didn't say anything to me. I
was in school that afternoon when I heard he'd had a heart
attack in his sleep.

*

I told you that Grandma taught me slowly, but in fact, I was just a slow learner. At that time I couldn't see the world she was trying to show me, a world of both light and shadow. Indeed, the darkness seemed much darker in those days, an aberration that my Aunt Polly was all too willing to caution me about. She said Grandma Belle's grandmotherly side was probably all right for me to be around. Peculiar perhaps, but tolerable. At least when Belle was being Grandma she was *trying* to do the decent thing, you know, be a proper... something, said my aunt. But when Grandma was being Belle, I should be careful. I should come straight home and not look back — unless I wanted to turn into salt.

It seems that at least once a month, Grandma would come down with some sort of fever and this most amazing event would occur. Grandma would become Belle.

She would remove her grandmotherly clothes and her grandmotherly hair. She would put on a red dress, bright red lipstick, patent leather heels and a black wig. (During these episodes, she stored her shawl in a closet — the only time I ever saw her without it.) Grandma would disappear and in her place would be this sort of whorey-goddess, who, loaded with an awesome range of psychic abilities and a half pint of whiskey, would take off down the railroad tracks in the direction of town. All my aunt or anyone could do was to call ahead and alert the sheriff that she was headed that way.

Once there, Belle would wander up and down the streets prophesying, healing, providing names for newborns, predicting the weather, warning strangers about difficult or dangerous times; she might even confess your life in front of everyone — what you were doing and who you were doing it to. No secret was safe. I wasn't privy to what else she might do, but I'd heard the rumors.

On those occasions in which Grandma was being Belle, she pretty much ignored me. That was fine with me. That was perfect. I didn't really want to be identified with Belle when she was being a goddess, or a whore. In those days I was very concerned that I at least *appear* to be normal — whatever that is. Looking back on it, I think Belle understood that about me. I had a weak soul and she knew it, and chose not to embarrass me for it.

She would eventually pass out, whether from too much whiskey or too much of the Holy Spirit, it was hard to say. She would lie down and go to sleep in the park, or down the alley, in the back of someone's pickup, wherever she was when the spirit left her. Usually someone would find her and take her home, leaving her asleep in her own front yard. And she claimed to have no memory of it the next day.

But I'm not so sure.

I think she knew more about the verities of her own soul than any of us realized or were willing to admit. After one particularly outrageous evening, I stopped by to see if she and Smokey were okay. I asked about her night out on the town. She was being Grandma again, but she winked and said, we certainly gave them their money's worth, didn't we?

Then she cautioned me about running off all my demons, lest I run off all my angels as well. A woman, she said, would rather have one measure of debauchery than ten of modesty. What is Eve without a serpent? What is God without Lucifer? Adam is always naked, Lot is drunk with his daughter, and the Messiah is always coming. She said, of course you know that words of light have no light in them, and wisdom is most certainly wise and righteous and full of itself, but love is unclean and holy.

I moved back to town the next year and didn't see much of Grandma Belle after that. But I was with her when she died. I was in Arizona at the time, in jail in Tucson when she suddenly appeared to me. In the time it takes to snap a photo, I saw her come into the yard and bend down and grab a fat hen from the flock of chickens around her feet and stick it under her arm and twist its neck with a kind of tenderness while she looked me square in the eye and told me that I think too much and don't eat well, stay for dinner, she said, tempting me with the strangled chicken she held with both hands so that it wouldn't get away and splatter blood everywhere. Then she turned and walked back to the house and was joined by Prune who was dressed like an usher. Together they paused at the door and looked back at me, then went inside, leaving the door standing open. By that, I knew to follow them.

She'd had a massive stroke and wasn't expected to live out the night. Only minutes apart but two hundred miles away, Donnie was dying of cancer. Not really sure what, but the two of them seemed to be one thing.

I came into the hospital room without being noticed. It was a black night in early October. The room was hot. She said, *wrap me in something.* I found her shawl and wrapped it around and around her like the sloughed skin of an insect. *Cover my face*, she said. I covered her face then stepped back from the lumpy shape on the bed and watched her slip away downstream — an Egyptian mummy bound in gauze, set in a boat and pushed out on the water, given over to the gods of the next world who may or may not find her.

All that was so long ago it seems like another lifetime. Maybe two. I've been declared dead twice since then. Still, not a day goes by that I don't take off all my clothes, everything, and dance in a circle in the woods.

*

Grandma's Shawl
{^}

Never one to smoke grapevines with the guys, I was, however, curious about Grandma Belle's pipe. How else can you know what's good for you, if you don't try some of what's not? So I stole a smoke from Grandma's pipe. In doing so, I also got tangled up in her shawl — a sort of double jeopardy.

Listen: Grandma Belle had been weaving that shawl for as long as anyone could remember. It was an epic. Woven from thread the color of night in late November, it was her idea to weave an entire world into that shawl. She had already woven stars, dark, cities, and weather into it, as well as an adventure story in which everything that could happen, did happen, but nothing 'timely' ever took place — she didn't trust time, didn't really believe in it.

So we're sitting around in the yard one afternoon and she's educating me, telling me things like: to be wise it to be the footstool for the beautiful and strong, angels can't read or write, and God himself, is empty-headed; she tells me that wisdom extends no further than the first heaven — everything after that is mystery or lust, one can never be sure. She's saying stuff like that, and smoking her pipe, blowing giant smoke clouds into the sky then weaving them into her shawl: smoke clouds in the shape of brooms, sailboats, flocks of sheep, herds of elephant, one cloud in the shape of a '55 Chevy, and another that looked like Jonah and the whale — her 'alien abduction story' she called it, though I wasn't sure at the time what she meant. But the camel-shaped cloud is the one that caused me concern. I was intrigued by camels because of their ability to store water in their humps, enough to last them for weeks. Grandma Belle told me that once, in a previous life, she'd been able to do that same thing by storing the water in her mind.

Sometimes she made me nervous when she talked like that. Sometimes I think she smoked too much. Her pipe smelled like a burnt rope. But something in the smoke or the words or her weaving caused me to be almost sick with curiosity. I felt green around the gills, but knew to keep quiet. Clouds, camels, smoke and curiosity, I watched Grandma weave them all into her shawl.

That evening I stole into Grandma's house. While she was out ravaging the neighborhood in her red outfit and black wig, I took her pipe from the dresser and let myself into her closet.

I'd never seen anything like it. Grandma's shawl was *everywhere*. I wrapped myself in it, lit her pipe, and inhaled. After that, I cannot be held responsible.

I took a long deep breath and inhaled all the daylight. Darkness spread.

I held my breath and the shawl became a desert after dark. I became a camel looking at the stars in wonder, with Prune disguised as a Bedouin nomad sitting on my back, cooled by the waters in my hump. Disguised as a camel, I watched a war

65

flare up violently, briefly engulf the world, and disappear. I glimpsed into the chaos: saw the earth tipped on its axis; saw cities, streets, and people disappear; saw animals, birds, bees, and trees disappear; earth, fire, water, here and there, all disappear. Unable to hold my breath any longer, I let out a long sigh and a breath of smoke, and from my great hairy nostrils came the morning. I saw the morning brighten into midday and midday burn across the sand dunes as cave men and dinosaurs reappeared, petals filled with syrup, green juices shot up into stems and leaves. I continued to exhale until prayer councils and rain dances came back and the tribal stage came and went, the hive instinct reappeared in primates, and cities reappeared, and smog reappeared, sin and guilt were reinvented; even as the sun burned its way across the shawl toward late afternoon, technology, crime, and clitoral politics were on the rise. A light tap from the nomad's/Prune's stick and I began to breathe the light back in until it was night again. Seven times I puffed on Grandma's pipe and seven times the world chaos took form, held its breath, and dissolved, while I stood there in the desert with the dreaming Prune on my back.

I put the pipe down and stood there in Grandma Belle's closet, wrapped in Grandma's shawl. I had the strange sensation that the earth I stood on was somehow a part of my skin; that I had never come into this world, but *out* of it, the way a leaf comes out of a tree. I stood there for what seemed like a very long time wondering if maybe I'd done permanent damage to myself. Not sure if it was the pipe or the shawl, I abandoned both right there, quit the closet, ran out of the house, and didn't stop running until I was home and in my own room, my own bed.

Still sick and worried, I got out of bed and knelt down and did an imitation of someone praying, very loud and for a long time. Then I did an imitation of someone being given absolution. Finally I crawled into bed, pulled the covers up under my chin, and lay there staring at the ceiling. I felt a little better about myself. There was a water stain on the ceiling that looked like a face attached to a long neck, skinny shoulders, and a pair of large breasts. I fell asleep and dreamed Arlene.

*

Arlene's Breasts
{^}

I became aware of Arlene in the fourth grade. She'd probably been there all along, but it wasn't until the fourth grade that I noticed her.

She was a big girl, quiet and shy. She wore her sister's hand-me-downs and always had a ribbon of snot hanging from her lip. She made poor grades, had no friends, and didn't talk at all; in fact, she didn't respond to questions in class, refusing to even answer the roll except by a tentative wave of her hand. Her features were large but not uncomely. And she had this huge mop of auburn brown hair that seemed to have never been cut or combed. Actually she might have been pretty under different circumstances. I could see that. Donnie must've seen it too, though it was not something we ever discussed.

Now that I think of it, she might have been a few years older than the rest of us. She was certainly more developed than the other girls, and never quite fit into the clothes of her older but smaller sister. Boys said naughty things to her and she kicked them in the balls. That was the only form of expression you could count on from Arlene. Only once had I ever seen her smile, and that, after delivering a particularly killing blow to Jimmy, causing him to throw up and swear to whip her brother's ass the first time he caught him off school grounds. It was a hollow threat; she had *six* brothers, all older, bigger, meaner than us. Anyway, I heard what Jimmy said to her; saw what he did. He deserved to have his balls kicked so far up inside him the nurse had to help get them down. Later he confessed that it was almost worth it, if the nurse hadn't been such a scary creature herself.

But I liked Arlene. At least I didn't dislike her. I certainly didn't tease her the way the other boys did. And the girls were even more cruel. I stayed out of all that. So did Donnie. In fact, he even went out of his way to be nice to her. I didn't have that kind of courage, but he was never one to care what people were saying or thinking. He always did what he felt like doing in that moment, and he was usually right.

By the time we were in the seventh grade, someone had taught Arlene how to wipe her nose and put on lipstick. It made a difference. Her grades got better. She began to talk, some, not a lot. Her social graces improved, though she still wasn't all that popular and didn't seem to care. In all the years I'd known her we had never exchanged more than a nod of hello. At least she didn't look on me as a threat, and I didn't have to worry about getting my voice kicked up an octave for looking at her wrong.

Nevertheless, Arlene was responsible for my first sexual experience — and a whole lot more than that. It happened like this:

My hometown is small and looks like something you might find on a postcard. The town itself sits in a natural bowl, surrounded by bluffs and hills. The main street is shaped like a "Z" and built along the banks of Sager Creek. There is a park on each end of town and a dam in one of the parks, otherwise the creek would just slide by and not even notice the town was there. But the creek and the dam are another story. This is about one of the springs in one of those parks, and me and Arlene and sex, sort of.

This was on a Saturday afternoon, the first really hot day of the summer. The town was filled with people, most of whom only came to town on Saturdays: people shopping, visiting, strolling in the parks, drinking iced tea, eating bucket loads of fried chicken, all that. Arlene and her family were there somewhere. I saw her brothers on the other end of town. I'd been zipping around on my bicycle, working up a thirst. I stopped at the park below the dam to get a drink from the spring, Twin Springs, enclosed on the sides, open overhead and down a dozen concrete steps, barely visible until you walk up on it. I parked my bicycle and went down the steps. It was mossy and cool down there. Arlene was sitting beside one of the springs, her bare feet dangling in the water.

She was alone.

We nodded hello to each other.

I bent down and cupped my hands in the cold water, drinking and splashing my face and neck. I stayed bent over that way for a long time, longer than was necessary, longer than was comfortable. I wanted to do what she was doing, take my sneakers off and put my feet in the water. But that meant we'd probably have to speak, maybe even engage in conversation. And I didn't have a clue as to how to go about that.

What happened next would change my life forever. To this day, thinking back on this incredible incident, I wonder if it could actually have occurred.

When I looked up from the spring, Arlene was looking me square in the eye. She had sweat beads on her forehead and upper lip. She was wearing a blue work shirt; sweat had formed two chevrons between her breasts. This next thing was beyond my wildest imaginings.

She opened her shirt and exposed her breasts.

Both of them! All of it! My god, she was bare-breasted and looking right at me. She may have been smiling. I had never seen a girl's naked breasts before, except in pictures or attached to a cousin. This was entirely different than a picture in a magazine. Entirely different.

I couldn't speak or breathe.

It was a dangerous moment, one in which I saw my whole life pass before my eyes, even the parts I hadn't lived yet. I considered the consequences of throwing myself off a cliff or in front of a car. Don't get me wrong, I am eternally grateful for that moment, despite all that happened later.

I suffered a temporary loss of sanity induced by a rush of testosterone to the brain. In that same moment in which I realized that I would do almost anything to get into Arlene's body, I was suddenly thrown *out* of my own. I underwent a religious conversion of sorts, *brranging* around the universe in search of answers or solutions or a more convivial God than the one I had been led to believe existed. Her breasts were *huge*! Large enough to have their own moons orbiting around them.

I couldn't help myself.

God couldn't help me.

I had an instant of clarity and knew, for better or worse, whatever happened next would be no one's fault but my own.

The sun was directly overhead, hot as blue blazes. I wanted to tell her about the sun and the spring and the shade and how grateful I was to her for having such a perfect mouth, such perfect lips, such teeth and tongue and hair and eyes. I wanted to tell her that I loved her and would die for just one...anything. I wanted with all my heart to reach out and touch her perfect body.

But in that moment in which so much was possible, so much hanging in the balance, I couldn't think of what next to do. And all I could think to say was, *Tits!*

She smiled and took a deep breath.

I said, *Knockers!*

Then I heard a crowd of voices approaching. I shot out of there, jumped on my bicycle, and headed for somewhere, anywhere. Home. I sped across the park, down Broadway, up Main, past the Spot Theater, past Bynum's Grocery, up the hill, past the ice plant and the poultry plant and the milk plant; I crossed the tracks, turned down the driveway, dumped my bike at the porch and headed for the pasture and the woods beyond. Three miles in twenty minutes.

I sat down beside the creek to catch my breath.

Then I took off all my clothes and slipped into the cool water. It was shallow, just deep enough to submerge my body stretched out on the gravel bottom. I lay there for a while, further romanticizing my moment with Arlene.

Then I crawled onto the bank and lay back in the mossy grass and fell asleep, or something like it.

I have no idea how long I slept or if sleep is what I was doing, but when I opened my eyes I seemed to be in a classroom with hundreds of others like myself, all of us buzzing around, talking, anticipating what was about to happen next. We seemed to know. I knew. We were in a giant planetarium — I mean, a planetarium the size of the *world*. Wherever you looked, some historical/cosmic event was being played out on the ceiling; you just had to shift your focus to see it.

Then the ceiling got wavy, like looking at it under water, a clear pool into which someone drops a stone, causing it to ripple out from the center in all directions. Form began to break up. All form. Every thing everywhere seemed to be turning into frequencies of colored light. For a moment the world was upside down and I was looking *up* at the ocean. Someone was rowing a boat in the ocean overhead. My whole body and all my consciousness seemed to be moving from one plane of existence into another. At first I thought I was going to throw up, then I thought I was going to cum — so pleasurable, so ecstatic, so...so *much* that I had to close my eyes just to keep the pleasure within tolerable limits.

And when I opened them again, it was over.

I've had a similar experience a number of times since, and always I close my eyes right there, missing whatever it is that is so wonderful I'm not even allowed to register it in consciousness. It's like trying to track the exact moment of an orgasm — one moment you're thinking, *not yet, not yet,* and the next instant you're in a free fall slide right through the gates of heaven. I opened my eyes and had already passed through some sort of gateway into a different world.

Someone familiar, someone I know now but didn't know then, was on screen spreading all our stars out in front of us, a sight such as I have never seen before or since, all our destinies pieced together like a puzzle/mandala the size of the universe. Just for an instant. Then it was gone. The mandala broke into a billion tiny pieces flying apart in all directions. After that it seemed to be my job to piece them back together from what I could remember.

The next time I woke up I was beside the creek and it was raining; one of those sudden rains that happen around here in summer, short and steamy; about all they do is turn the air into soup. But they are wonderful and refreshing for the few minutes they're happening. For just an instant, I felt like someone was watching me, had, in fact, been watching me for quite some time. The hair on the back of my neck stood up and a chill rippled through my body.

Then it was gone.

I was alone. I was naked. I felt exhausted but really good. I thought about Arlene. I didn't know *what* to think about the rest of it. And because I didn't know what to think or where to put it, it began immediately to fall out of my memory. I wouldn't remember any of it for years. And not until now would I remember it all together.

*

Later that summer, Arlene and Donnie were caught swimming in a muddy pool at the end of Black Road. The sheriff, my uncle, heard someone giggling in the weeds and looked to see what it was. It was Donnie and Arlene, naked as two earthworms. The first chance I got, I asked Donnie about it but all he ever said was, *she knew stuff.*

God! how I wanted to know *what* stuff. I wanted to know what stuff in the worst way. But I wasn't about to admit to my own shenanigans with Arlene. What I told Donnie was that she had actually been responsible for a sexual experience of my own several weeks earlier. (Never mind that she wasn't actually there at the time it occurred, she was certainly responsible for it.) A few months later Donnie confessed that she had taken him places he had not previously known existed. He wouldn't elaborate, but I think I know what he meant. And I think Donnie probably knew my story too, but he didn't try to embarrass me with it.

And that fall Arlene began wearing dresses to school. She was hopelessly in love with Donnie and determined to press her affections on him at any cost. She carried his books between classes, sat by him in study hall, cleared his lunch tray away, and offered to kick the ass of anyone whose ass Donnie wanted kicked. Just point them out, she said. I'll make dog shit out of them. And once at a school function, a girl tried to dance with Donnie, only to have Arlene drag her off the floor by the hair.

Donnie was flattered but nonplussed. He did nothing to encourage her attentions. I don't mean to say he was mean or insulting. He wasn't at all. It's just that he did nothing to encourage her. That only aggravated her condition. It was a practice Donnie put to good use again and again for all of his abbreviated life. He was delighted by women. He was amazed and confused by women. Stupidly charming and genuinely innocent, Donnie had a gift. By the time he was sixteen so many little girls were climbing through his window at night that it was rumored the Girl Scouts were actually giving a patch for it.

Arlene kept up her assault for the better part of that semester. Meanwhile, her wardrobe changed. She replaced her blue jeans with dresses and her T-shirts with halter-tops. She eventually learned to walk like a lady, sort of; at least she walked less like a cowboy. But she refused to concede much more than that. By the end of the semester she had given up on

Donnie as an object of romance. But not as a friend. They never stopped being bawdy and raunchy friends to one another. I envied them that. I never stopped envying the two of them.

By the time we were in the ninth grade, Arlene was in full bloom. Big and brassy and bosomy, she was on the verge of becoming beautiful and didn't know it. She still ate with her mouth open, talked with her mouth full, snored in class, and worked beside her brothers in the fields with no shirt on, no bra, nothing. I never actually saw her like that myself, but that same someone I didn't know earlier/Prune did. He rode behind her riding topless on a tractor all one rainy spring afternoon. He swore to it, and I can imagine it.

What more can I say? Arlene, the planetarium-of-world-events, the shattered mandala, all of it caused my whole world to turn over in ways I have only just begun to appreciate. I've seen the planetarium a few times since. Not sure if it's an out-of-body-experience, something from a parallel existence, or a dream, plain and simple. Not really sure what I believe. But I do know this: four decades later, at a certain time of day in a certain season and always unexpectedly, all I have to do is think of Arlene and I become some sort of Manchurian Candidate, triggered into a series of events for which I have no control, and teleported to some place deep and beyond even my own belief system; a place from which I always come back amazed, perplexed, and wonderfully spent.

*

Close Encounter
{^}

Not long after the breast-thing with Arlene, something else happened that was even more amazing.

It must have been a Friday night, early in November. Donnie was sleeping over, and it was a few days after Halloween. Out in the pasture, sometime after midnight, a bright ball of fire drifted down the sky along a curious course, down, down, slowly toward the earth. I watched it for what seemed like a long time above the woods at Buffalo Park. Just over the gypsy camp the fireball seemed to explode. Sparks looking like shooting stars went off in all directions then drifted harmlessly into the trees. There was no thunder, no lightning. The sky was as clear and bright as I'd ever seen it.

Donnie and I had plans to hike out to Lake Francis the next day and explore the cave at Lookout Point. In anticipation, we'd gone to bed early. He went right to sleep, something I've never been able to do. I tossed and turned, slept a little, dreamed a little, woke up, off and on all night. Have you ever dreamed you were awake and when you woke up you were asleep? Well, that's what the entire night was like.

77

For three days the wind had been blowing out of the north, stripping trees, rattling windows, pushing dark clouds ahead of it. I was awake, listening to all that when the train from Kansas City pulled onto the spur at the Pet Milk Plant adjacent to our property. That was just before midnight. It belched and blew steam into the night air. For another hour I listened to it couple and uncouple, pull forward and backward again and again, dropping one car, picking up another.

Then it was quiet for a while. And I slept.

Then it whistled, sharp and shrill, and pulled away sounding like a giant bone yard of smoke stacks and flywheels and drive shafts and melded bolts gathering itself into one thing, then down the tracks, across the trestle bridge, and into the night. Leaving, it seemed to take the wind and clouds with it. Suddenly everything got very still and very bright.

Not long after that, the fireball exploded over the gypsy camp.

Amazing, I said to myself. *What a night*!

From the cot across the room, Donnie scarcely seemed to breathe.

Are you asleep? I said

Yes.

How could you be?

I'm asleep.

Have you seen what's going on outside?

No.

I've never seen any thing like it.

He didn't answer. He didn't move. I wondered if perhaps he had died. Of course I knew better, but it was that kind of a night.

I'm going out there. Do you want to go with me?

No.

Let's sneak up on the gypsy camp.

Uh huh.

C'mon, let's go see what the gypsies are up to. See if they really do what Uncle Gark says they do all night.

Uh huh.

I'm going.

Okay, he said.

Then he turned over on his stomach and buried his face in the pillow.

I got up. The linoleum floor felt like ice on a pond. My jeans were stiff from the cold. There was no moon to speak of, but flashes of starlight were everywhere in the room. Outside I could see, almost as if it were daytime, the meadow, the creek, the woods, even the smoke from the gypsy camp, or so I thought. Maybe not the smoke. But I could see everything else. Our pasture lay between the railroad tracks and the Pet Milk Plant on one side, and Buffalo Park on the other. The night was luminous and everywhere.

I let myself out the backdoor, quietly, trying not to awaken my Aunt Juliet sleeping in the front bedroom. Crossing the yard I felt Smokey at my heels. Smokey was not my dog but he didn't know he was not my dog. He actually belonged to Grandma Belle, but most of his time was spent following me around. Part shepherd and part collie, Smokey looked like a wolf, a city wolf, said my uncle; he was too fat and friendly to be wild. He followed me across the yard without a sound. Whatever was in the air, he was feeling it too. Janet mooed once, and gave it up.

I opened the wide iron gate. It gave directly onto the pasture.

There was no moon, but the sky seemed to be scattered with hot coals. The air smelt of ashes. I wondered if that had anything to do with the fireball. It did seem to come from the direction of the gypsy camp. The gypsies camped in Buffalo Park, a wooded area scattered with scrub oak, squatty cedars, a few willows growing along upper Sager Creek. I don't know why it was called Buffalo Park. If there had ever been buffalo around here they were long since gone. Now it was simply the place where gypsies camped while they worked the harvests. The creek was clear and cold but narrow and not very deep, its banks lined with berries and moss and clover and all manner of soft grasses. A good place to camp.

Smokey and I set out across the field in that direction. There was so much light against the deep shadows and eerie colors, I could not remember ever seeing the world that way before.

If it's to happen at all, I thought, it will happen on a night like this. Not knowing who or what that meant.

For a long time I had been expecting something or someone to arrive and....do...*something.* I had an abundance of religious fervor in those days, left over from three generations of evangelism, I guess. But that didn't seem to be it. There was the Moon and Venus and things going on in my dreams that I couldn't talk to anyone about. There was Jimmy and Donnie and Arlene. There was Grandma Belle and all that. It had to add up to something. But what? A desire for something I didn't know existed? An expectation of something I could not name? Perhaps it was 'the mother ship,' or the Second Coming. I just knew that somewhere, perhaps around the next corner or through the next door or because of the next stranger, my life was going to change. At the edge of the pasture, I climbed the fence and Smokey found a way under. He was staying close. Normally he'd be chasing critters by now, possum, skunk, raccoon; there were weasels out there too, and deer. But he'd have none of it. It was another hundred yards to the edge of the woods and we crept along in the tall grasses.

At the creek I crossed over on some stones, but he didn't trust that. He whined and ran up and down the bank before finally slipping into the icy waters. He swam across, crawled out and shook himself. We walked into the woods, to the spot where the flames seemed to fall. I thought I might see a spark somewhere along the ground, or in the branches of a tree. But there were no traces, no scorching, nothing. We were close enough to the gypsy camp that I thought I heard voices. I thought I heard a flute.

It must have been three o'clock in the morning.

The ground was covered with dead leaves. I lay down in the leaves and Smokey lay down beside me. Together we planned our next move. I decided that he should stay behind while I crept as close to the camp as I could. He didn't think that was a good idea. I told him to *Stay*! But he ignored me.

Together we inched our way forward, crawling through the leaves.

About fifty yards from where I knew the camp to be, we stopped, crouching behind a boulder that jutted out into the creek. I could see all I wanted to from there.

I don't know what I expected: bright painted wagons drawn up around a huge fire, I guess; and horses grazing nearby, old men smoking pipes and playing fiddles and flutes and Jew's-harps while young women with long dark hair and painted eyes danced and flirted with the young men and the old men and the sheep and the fire and....I'd have been better off living with my expectations.

This was nothing like that. This was like an old movie, silent, and done in black-and-white. At first I thought everybody was dead.

There were a half dozen tents scattered around, six or eight old cars and trucks, mostly Fords and Chevrolets, one old Packard. There was a chuck wagon made from a pickup with what looked like a wooden outhouse built on top of it. Two of the trucks had their hoods raised, greasy parts lying everywhere, a puddle of oil in the grass. There was a goat and a mule, some chickens tied together, and a rain barrel. No evidence of a fireball. The air around the camp smelled sweet and smoky, but the campfire had gone out. All I saw of people were unlaced boots sticking out from under tent flaps. It didn't look fun or romantic. It certainly didn't look sexy. It just looked hard and desperate. Maybe my recollection is faulty. Maybe I got there too late; perhaps there was a curfew and the party broke up earlier. Mostly I didn't want these people to catch me spying on their private stuff. I started planning a secret retreat, how to get Smokey and me both out of there without getting caught.

That's what I was doing when a voice came out of the dark behind me *What are we looking for?*

Holy Shit! I cried. And managed to jump, slip, and fall full-length into the creek. A hand reached out swiftly and pulled me up by the hair. I stood sputtering, dazed and dumbfounded, up to my knees in icy waters, wondering if perhaps this was to be my last day on earth.

Which it was, and it wasn't.

Recalling what happened next, my memory could be faulty, even contradictory. Some of the details might be exaggerated, and some could be wrong. It was all so dreamlike. I wasn't sure what to do. I thought about running. But I wasn't sure how far I could get. Caught, dead to rights. I thought about apologizing, but before I could get very far with that, whoever it was — a man, that's all I knew for certain — stepped into the water, took me by the elbow, and assisted me onto the bank.

Didn't mean to frighten you, he said.

Are you with them? I asked, indicating the gypsy camp.

No, he said. Are you?

No. I was just meaning to.... But then, I couldn't really explain what it was I was meaning to do.

It doesn't matter, he said. We'd better dry you off. And with that he led me deeper into the woods, away from the gypsy camp, to where he had a fire already going. Just a short distance from here, he said. He paused to light a pipe but I didn't get a look at his face. I couldn't tell how old he was or what he looked like. Whatever he was smoking smelled really foul.

What do you think of this night? he said.

I can't remember ever seeing one like it.

It *is* unusual, he said. The Seven Sisters are all decked out for winter. And I don't know that I've ever seen Sirius looking quite so bright, almost animated.

What?

Sirius. It's especially bright. There. Do you see it?

No.

Too bad, he said. "I expect you will. You'll see a great deal of Sirius in your lifetime.

His own campsite looked abandoned. I don't recall there being any camping stuff, no clothing, no sleeping gear, nothing, except a perfect fire. I remember thinking that I'd never before seen a campfire that looked so...right. I sat down on a perfect rock beside that perfect fire and began warming myself.

Then I remembered Smokey. *What happened to my dog?*

That's a fine animal you've got there, he said. Not much of a guard dog, I'm afraid. But a really handsome creature.

Where'd he go?

My guess is, he's almost home by now.

And sure enough, Smokey had jumped the creek, jumped the fence, and was halfway back to the house before I ever climbed out of the water. I don't know why he didn't hear something or smell something or in some way sound an alarm. I thought they were supposed to know things like that.

He'll be all right, said the man. He'll rejoin us later.

You think so?

I'm sure of it.

As soon as he said that, I let go of it. I turned back to the fire, warming my hands and feet. Strangely enough, from the inside, my clothes felt almost dry. All things considered, I was quite comfortable.

You're not from around here, are you? I said.

Yes. And no. If you're asking if I'm local, not really. However, from time to time I do visit a place in the mountains not far from here. With his pipe he traced a line in the night toward the east. A place called Shaeburg, he said. But I doubt you've heard of it.

And I hadn't. Not yet, at least.

Anyway, I was in the area, saw the train coming this way and thought I'd come with it.

You came on the train?

No.

I understand, I said.

No, you don't.

He smoked as we talked; moving around, first on one side of the fire, then on the other, then into the shadows, back into the light again. He appeared to be tall and thin from one angle, short and heavy from another. His hair was curly or stringy, light or dark, I couldn't tell. He sounded older than he looked, but then, he could've been any age from fifteen to fifty. And his words kept falling out of my ears before I was through with them. I missed a lot. My head was spinning. And there was that damned pipe.

What is that you're smoking? It smells awful.

It does, doesn't it. I'm not sure what it is, he said. Someone left it on that log over there. I figured they weren't coming back for it.

I can understand why.

"Yes, you can," he said, and seemed satisfied with some thought of his own.

So, why did you come *here*? I asked. This place exactly?

Coincidence, he said. Strictly by coincidence at first. Then it was the train and the weather. But not now. Now it is by design. Things are like that, you know. Decided without our understanding why. Then we do them and think we've done something."

I see, I said.

No, you don't.

No, I don't, I said. And I didn't. I didn't see or understand a damn thing that was going on, or a word that had been spoken since I climbed out of the creek. I didn't know who this stranger was, what he was, what he looked like, or what in fact we were doing here together. I was beginning to get a little pissed off at everything I didn't know.

I saw you sneaking up on something, he said. I said to myself: What do you suppose he's sneaking up on! So I came to see.

Yes, I said, but it wasn't just the gypsies. It was something else, sort of. Did you see that fireball in the sky? It was that, or something, made me want to...do *something*. Do you know what I mean?

He laughed softly. Yes, I do know what you mean. But do *you* know what you mean? Then he nodded at another private thought of his own and took a big puff on his pipe. And this is certainly a good night for it.

For what, I asked?

Whatever it is, he said.

My head was beginning to hurt, either from the pipe he smoked or the things he said or didn't say. I wasn't sure then and I'm not sure now.

He stopped talking for a while and stood at the edge of the light with his back to the fire, looking up at that amazing night sky. Then he began to whistle. I didn't recognize the tune but it seemed to be in harmony with everything else going on: the wind, the clouds, the train coming and going, the quiet afterward, and then the fireball, even the gypsies were in there somewhere. He whistled softly, between his lips, each tone flawless and round, going into all the right places. It sounded like the flute I'd heard earlier. He whistled for himself and for me. Like a secret between us.

Something inside me moved, maybe it broke, I'm not sure.

I thought I might cry — for no reason, for every reason. I felt an overwhelming urge to tell him something, or explain something, or perhaps invent something to confess. This next was really difficult:

Have you ever...? I mean, do you think...? If...if you... But I couldn't say it. I couldn't even find words to describe what was in my mind.

Not really, he said. Maybe. Once with my mother when I was very small, and another time when I was visiting a cousin in the Ukraine. If I did I certainly wouldn't feel guilty about it. And I'd probably do it again should the opportunity arise. Then he passed very close but without actually touching me.

It's all in the mind, you know. Just because you think of a lake, doesn't mean your head fills up with water. Then he stepped back and looked at me as though he had just invented me, and didn't know what to call his invention. Do you understand?

I don't think so.

Excellent, he said.

Then he began whistling again. Whatever he was whistling, Smokey must have heard it, too. He slipped quietly into camp and parked himself beside me. He put his wet nose in my hand. Normal sensation was moving back into my body for the first time since I'd climbed out of the creek. I felt a little chilled. Smokey lay down beside me and the stranger lit another pipe and sat down across from us.

I wanted to know where did he come from? Where was he headed? And how did he end up here? How long did he intend to stay? Where was he going next? I asked him what his name was.

Prune, he said.

What? I said.

My name is Prune, he said — not because that was his name, but because no one could pronounce his real name. That's what he told me. So Prune it was. (And Prune it is. That's what I've called him for almost forty years.)

He was a little fuzzy about where he came from. But he came to be here because this is where he was headed. He planned to stay as long as it took. And he had no idea where he'd be going next.

So you're looking for work, I said.

No, he said.

What do you do?

What do I do, he said, and I could see him thinking about it. Well, for example, I can do this.

He wiggled his ears, arched his eyebrows, scrunched his face up something terrible, and swallowed his nose. My god, I thought, I wish I could do that. Then he swallowed his ears. His head looked like a bowling ball with eyes and long hair. Then he twisted his legs up real funny and put both feet in his pockets, stuck his head between his knees and walked around the campfire on his hands. That, I did not want to do. Then he took his feet out of his pockets but left his legs folded up and walked around looking like a dwarf. He couldn't have been over three feet tall. I was amazed. Overwhelmed. A little sick to my stomach. He unfolded himself and stood upright.

A bit extreme, he said, but maybe you get the picture.

I was stunned, stoned, unable to think, speak or move. I may have been a little feverish.

And while we're at it, he said, there is also this.

He took off his coat. Beneath his coat he wore a dark blue jacket with shiny gold buttons and a badge. He took off his trousers. Uh oh, I thought, here it is! Queer assault! Queer assault! I prepared to fight or flee. Under his trousers was another pair of trousers, matching his blue jacket. From somewhere he pulled out a dark blue cap with a bill. My god, he was a policeman!

He whistled.

He raised his hand in the air and laughed softly.

Then he removed the blue jacket and underneath that was a buckskin shirt. He took off his blue pants and underneath was a pair of buckskin pants On his head was some sort of beaded headband with a feather. He whistled again, did a cartwheel into the dark and came back into the light wearing a long silk robe with a sash. He disappeared into the dark again and came back wearing a pair of khaki shorts, a pith helmet and a Hawaiian sport shirt. He kept going.

I wasn't afraid exactly, but I did wonder where all this was leading. Where are we since the train and the fireball? Where are we since the gypsies? And where since Sirius and the whistling?

He became more bold. Without changing his expression, his voice, or his clothes, he transformed himself into some sort of prophet or soothsayer, then he turned into a priest, and after that a poet, an old man, a young woman, a child, a deer, a pond; he became the king of something, the queen of something else. There seemed to be no end. While one of his faces was up in the chapel talking to God, another was entertaining thought of becoming a sinner. He disguised himself as a lawyer, a thief, a cowboy, a clown, a cocktail and a waitress. A shape-shifter of glorious proportions, he took off everything but a loincloth and sat on the ground with his legs crossed and his eyes crossed. He took a deep breath and expelled the air. It was not the respiration of anything I'd ever heard, certainly nothing human.

What happened next is a mystery. I say that, because what he turned into was so awesome and unbelievable that it knocked me flat out. I have no recollection whatsoever.

I fell asleep and dreamed that something religious was being done to me: Naked, I was taken into a lush green forest and made to stand under a waterfall of gold light while this most gorgeous divine-mother-queen-of-the-world-thing made love to me. She kissed me on the eyes. And on the nose. And on the mouth, everywhere, all over. I woke up and Smokey was licking my face.

And Prune was gone.

I didn't even bother to look for him. Truth is, I had only a fuzzy recollection of *anyone* else having been there. I woke up and Prune was out of sight and fast receding from memory. If not for what happened next, I'd probably have dismissed him altogether.

All those stars in all that sky were gone. The sky was actually green, like something sick or stormy was about to happen. Smokey and I walked up out of the woods and across the field. Donnie was swinging on the gate, waiting for us.

You didn't see no gypsies, did you?

Kinda, I said. Not really.

What've you been doing out there all night?

Walking, mostly. We built a fire.

You and who?

Me and Smokey.

Sure you did, he said, and laughed at something he thought he knew. You been with *him*, haven't you?

Who?

Him! *Prune*! You been with Prune. Did he throw you in the water? Did he baptize your ass? Did he teach you to whistle? Donnie could barely contain himself. Oh, you're gonna be a sick dog now.

I didn't want to hear it at the time, but of course he was right. on every count. I went to bed for a week. I had fever, chills. I had diarrhea. I had unbelievable dreams, one of which is running even now.

And I learned to whistle that night. Don't ask me how or to what purpose, but I've been able to whistle since. I'm very good at it. It's a handy skill to have should you be caught walking across a graveyard after dark.

And of course, forty years later Prune is still around. Sleeping by day, dreaming by night, alive and living in every thing I think or do, Prune continues to confound me by leaving a trail of prophecies that confuse my judgment and exhaust my will, prophecies that contradict one another but are, nonetheless, true, every damnable one of them, true. Sometimes a saint, sometimes a sinner, always a fool, a liar, a cheat, whatever in Mother-Father-God's own name that he is, Prune has become my Virgil: only he knows the way.

*

Tap Dancing With The Stars
{^}

The very first time I saw Fred Astaire dance across the silver screen I knew he was someone to be reckoned with, but not someone I wanted to be. His ears were too big and his legs too skinny. I wanted to be Gene Kelley. Of course, dancing with Ginger Rogers was worth some consideration. But then there was Cyd Charisse. She had really long legs. I remember watching her dance with Gene Kelley and kicking her foot so high it passed right across the top of his head. I wondered what he could see from there that I couldn't see from the front row of the Spot Theater.

There were definite advantages to being Gene Kelley. Still, my designs were more along the lines of the manly arts: football, basketball, track, things like that. I did not, at first, think tap-dancing lessons were such a good idea. That was girl stuff. What would my friends think? And if it was so good for your agility and coordination, why weren't Jimmy and Donnie doing it? If it was so sure to make me a better ballplayer, why had I never heard of any of my favorite players starting this way? My Mom and Dad were giving me a hard sell on how good this would be for my career, and what a wholesome way to spend the summer, and why didn't I withhold judgment for a few weeks, just give it a try and see.

Tap-dancing lessons were to be held each Saturday morning in the banquet room behind the Spot Theater. Nothing like this had ever been offered in Siloam so everyone would be starting new. It still sounded like sissy stuff to me. It was a setup, and I knew it, an attempt to get me situated before my momma and daddy went off on one last hoorah. They were going on an extended vacation to see if they could find love again, this time with each other.

That first Saturday morning I showed up in sneakers, without taps. (I wasn't about to make it easy on anyone.) There were twenty-five or thirty little girls of all ages, sizes and shapes; there were two old ladies, one old man, and myself. I was looking for a rear exit or an open window, some way out of there, when Deanna Winters arrived. Deanna was a senior in high school, she was a cheerleader, she was a roller derby queen, she was to be our dancing instructor.

Deanna's legs looked long to me, perhaps not as long as Cyd Charisse's but long enough. Her hips were slim, her lips were full, she wore her hair in a braid to her waist. What else she had would break any boy's heart.

It was settled then. My reasons for being there were moot. Everything was changed, pride meant nothing. Secret agendas were irrelevant. I cared not a whit what a sissy this would make of me. I had been delivered to my destiny. I would dance. I would marry Deanna. We would have five or six kids and live together forever. Deanna was the final answer to all doubt on every subject. She was beautiful. She was otherworldly. I wanted to kiss her all over though I wasn't sure I would know how to kiss if I had the chance. It did not matter that I had just committed myself to tap-dancing, the purview of girls and sissies; I was in love. That afternoon I had my brogans fitted for taps.

To be honest, I don't remember much about that first lesson, or the next. A couple of the little girls were actually cousins of mine but I did my best to avoid them. I talked to no one. Hung around with no one. Didn't like it when I was forced to team up with anyone. In my mind it was just Deanna and me. We were rehearsing for a lifetime together. It never occurred to me that had our ages been reversed I would have been considered a stalker. Had she felt about me the way I felt about her, it would not have been love, but a symptom of pathology.

On the Saturday of our third lesson it was raining, had been raining for days. Deanna's boyfriend drove her to class, then waited. I didn't like it when he did that. He seemed genuinely insensitive to how Deanna and I felt about each other. After the lesson I hung around, hoping to get a private word with her. I don't know what I intended to say, but I figured to invent something that would minimize the presence of her boyfriend. I thought about telling her I had been diagnosed with a terminal disease, or that my parents had been killed in an automobile accident that very morning. I'd think of something. I dawdled around taking off my brogans, putting on my sneakers, waiting for everyone else to clear out. I went down the hall and into the bathroom.

When I came out most of the lights were off and the hallway was dark. Deanna and her boyfriend were standing under the exit sign, the two of them barely visible in the neon light. They didn't notice me. I was suddenly aware of just how much more there is for a boy and girl to share beyond the act of kissing. It was awful, realizing how much some secrets could hide. They kissed. Then they touched each other and laughed. They did it again only this time they did not laugh, and they did not stop immediately. Furtively, I watched them fondle each other in the dark. I'm not sure if I was more upset by what he was doing to her or what she was doing to him.

In that instant I knew that all the ways I had of comprehending the world were no longer adequate. I was crushed. I felt betrayed, suicidal. I wanted to die a horrible death right in front of her. For the first time in my life I was driven to consider my own death in a real sense. It took me most of the afternoon to get over it.

I ducked out the rear exit to where my bicycle was parked. The rain had slacked off a little. I headed for home before the next wave of storms hit.

It had been raining for several days, almost without stop. The creek was on the rise, everything smelled swampy. I wondered if this was what the world of betrayal smelled like. I had no way of knowing, but every stream and gully for miles was gathering for a flood. No ordinary flood either. But a flashflood of new consciousness flooding the gardens and the gutters, filling the rain barrels, forcing toads up out of their homes and onto the highways. I had to be careful not to run over them as I sped through the wet streets.

When I got home, Aunt Juliet was down in the storm cellar. No one else was around. I parked my bike on the porch and went through the house. Looking out the kitchen window, our pasture had turned into a lake with a small island in the middle of it. The island was covered with animals, wild and domestic. Smokey was on the island barking at something. Janet was mooing. This is big, I thought. This is big enough to catch the eye of Deanna Winters.

Behind the tool shed at the edge of the lake was a barn door Donnie and I had stolen and turned into a raft by strapping logs to it. Three weeks earlier we had caused quite a stir by navigating Sager Creek through the middle of town, strictly forbidden. My uncle, the sheriff, reeled us in at the dam, and made us sit in a cell all afternoon just to see what it felt like to be a jailbird. (It felt fine.)

I pushed the raft into the water, poled my way out to the island and began taking live things on board, two by two: two dogs, two cats, two cows, two cousins, chickens, rats, goats and fleas, two hares in heat, and a pair of mountain lions that would not stop eating the sheep. You get the picture?

I was poling my way across the pasture on the barn door laden with all manner of live creatures when the floodwaters hit. I had just enough time to bury my pole in the mud then fell overboard trying to remove it.

I was immediately pulled under and swept away.

No time to catch one last breath, I was sucked down and away, into some watery corridor of time and space. And didn't come ashore until I was several centuries upstream, in Peru, of all places. I know that now, but at the time I didn't have a clue. In a life parallel to this one, I seemed to be keeping company with the son of some Big Guy. This Big Guy I now know to be Viracocha, storm-god of the Incas. Viracocha's son was dressed in rags, disguised as a shepherd from the highland caves. He was there to teach irrigation, terrace farming, the keeping of records, mystical arts, stuff like that. During his travels he saw and fell in love with a haughty young woman who was herself possessed of a divine spirit. She was of the highest earthly lineage and ignored him, thinking him to be a peasant. So, he assumed the guise of a bird and sat in a fruit tree outside her window. Noting that she ate from the fruit tree every day, he injected his sperm into the fruit, which she ate, and then became pregnant.

By now he was so distracted by his love for the young woman that he didn't remember who he was. She was equally distracted, outraged even, insisting that she was a virgin. But no one believed her. She continued to insist, even after she gave birth to a son. And she continued to reject the boy's father, causing him to become more distracted and less connected. He stopped teaching, lost his mystical abilities, and began working at odd jobs, doing menial labor just to be near the young woman and their son. Then one day, she took their son and moved away, just changed her name and disappeared altogether. The son of Virococha was beside himself. He was wandering through the market place inquiring as to her whereabouts when Prune, disguised as a peasant dressed in rags, came up and handed him a piece of fruit, a mango, I think it was. In that moment, he remembered who he was, remembered his past and why he had come here. In that same moment, I came awake feeling oddly between things. I had washed ashore on the grassy banks of the Illinois River in the northwest corner of Arkansas.

For the duration of that moment I was suddenly aware that I have total recall but in pieces, and out of time; so that I am unable to remember what I know or even that I know it. On the banks of the Illinois, with no idea who I was, where I was, or how I'd come to be there, I woke up. Smokey was there. Janet was there. My mother, my aunt, Donnie, Belle, and my grandmother were all there; Deanna was nowhere in sight, but two future wives, an unborn daughter, and a bunch of people I didn't recognize, all came running up to me: *Are you okay? That's the most amazing damned thing I ever saw. Are you sure you're all right?* I got to my feet, brushed myself off and looked around, nervously. Everything seemed to be crouched, waiting and eager to turn into something else.

*

Hoboes, Trains, and a Cave
{^}

There wasn't time to think it out very well. We came hiking around a bend in the tracks, saw the hoboes camped in a deep ravine and heard the train whistle somewhere in the mountains, not far. It was Jimmy's idea to toss a bee hive into the hobo camp then catch the train as it slowed down for the steep incline, and ride home — the tracks ran right across the backside of my Aunt Juliet's pasture. All the parts came together at once: we spotted the beehive about the same time we heard the train and saw the hoboes.

The first part of the plan went well, too well — a dozen angry hoboes running up and down the campsite, cursing, trying to figure out who would do such a thing, surely not one of their own. By the time they spotted us, the train was right on top of us, but it was going too fast, and in the wrong direction.

Too late to reconsider, we were committed to our original plan, good or bad.

It was a short train, a single engine, followed by a coal car, a couple dozen freight cars, a flatcar, and a caboose. The flatcar was empty and seemed like the best bet, so I sprinted up beside it, tossed my bedroll on board, then followed it as best I could, picking up a few splinters and tearing a hole in the knee of my pants; not bad, all in all. The train was picking up speed but Donnie was right behind me. Jimmy was another matter. Jimmy ran hard but he ran too long in one place. His legs were churning but he was still losing ground. In a last ditch effort, he attempted to hurl himself and his bedroll onto the train, managed to get a good grip on Donnie's outstretched hand, but couldn't pull himself up or get his feet moving fast enough, so he just hung there like a rag thing, picking up sparks and cinders, his sneakers bouncing off the gravel. Then the gravel dropped off abruptly and he was suspended in mid-air as the train crossed a trestle bridge, a fifty-foot drop into who knows what.

Anyone else would have passed out right there, but Jimmy shimmied up Donnie's arm like it was a flagpole. Then he passed out. And shit all over himself. Maybe he shit himself earlier. I don't know. But he certainly was a mess. And he'd managed to throw his bedroll clear over the flatcar.

So there we were, the three of us speeding down the tracks on a flatbed car, safe, kind of, and headed in the wrong direction. It was twenty miles before we were able to get off.

The train stopped in Westville. We bought Peanut Butter Logs and as much bread and bologna as we had money. Then hung around the switching yard for an hour, waiting for another train going in the opposite direction. It was easier this time. The train slowed down like it was supposed to, and we jumped off just before we got to the hobo camp.

We'd lost half a day and were right back where we started. Of course, all that was forty years ago and I don't remember what our original destination was, or if we even had one. Most of our 'experiences' were divinely inspired and thought up in the moment.

The idea was to camp somewhere along the river, get up early the next morning and spend the day exploring the cave at Lookout Point. So the river was first in our mind; from there we could find the cave; a campsite would present itself.

By dead reckoning, we made our way through swamp-lands, tangled underbrush, and densely wooded hills — mountains to us — toward where we thought the river should be. It was hot and muggy. Jimmy smelled awful, so we threw him in the creek with all his clothes on and made him walk behind us. He bitched about it. But then, he bitched about everything. (His bitching was like singing to Donnie and me, and we sang along with him.)

There was still plenty of light but it was getting late in the day, and we hadn't yet found the river. Just before dusk we stumbled onto a cabin. There were hundreds of cabins in these hills, up and down the river and around the lake; retreat cabins, built in the twenties and abandoned in the thirties when the banks went bust.

This one was empty, by the looks of it, had been empty for quite some time. But not entirely abandoned. There was firewood stacked outside, some of it green. The cabin was locked up, but you could see furniture through the windows. Varmints had gotten into the cabin by clawing and chewing through the screens on the back porch windows, their little feet making tracks in the dust. Jimmy got in the way the varmints got in, then went through the cabin and kicked the front door open, kicked it right off its hinges, kicked it off the porch and halfway down the mountain. I think it had something to do with him being short and all.

I was in favor of going on, and spending the night under the stars. But it was almost dark, it had been a full day, and Jimmy no longer had a bedroll. So we built a fire in the fireplace, pulled a mattress into the main room and slept there, three across. A good thing too, the cabin, I mean, because a squall blew up in the night, and it rained.

*

By the time Donnie and I woke up the next morning, Jimmy was already dressed and gone, struggling back up the side of the mountain with the front door. Without benefit of hammer or nails, he repaired it as best he could. But he couldn't attach the door to the frame so he just left it standing there, leaning against the hole, looking like a door.

From the porch in the morning light, we were able to catch a glimpse of the lake, and by that, knew how to find the river. We put the mattress back, cleaned up after ourselves, ate bologna sandwiches, and set out. By noon we were at Lookout Point and had only to cross the lagoon and climb the cliff face to get to the cave. The lagoon was a swampy backwater filled with snakes and folklore. Deep and dark, it was said to hold a standing forest just beneath its surface. More than once we had tried to goad one another into swimming across, but none of us had ever done it. There was a weathered rowboat pulled out of the water and turned bottom side up. Jimmy thought it looked like a good place to dump a body should the need arise, you know, anchor it with a rock then row out to the middle of the lagoon and toss it overboard. I wanted to know whose body did he have in mind. Maybe yours, he said, and looked as menacing as a really short guy can look.

Lookout Point sits on the face of a bluff, three hundred feet above the river. Once the site of a three-story house, a mansion, sort of, built in the twenties by the man who owned the bank in Siloam, who was, himself, owned by the Joplin mob. Or so I'm told. Listen: we're on the edge of the Cookson Hills; in the twenties and thirties this was still thought of as the badlands, a place where bandits and robbers could hide out without too much concern for local law enforcement, and no concern at all for the FBI—G-Men? Is that what they were called? It was a safe place, a party place, a place you could take your woman and do things you wouldn't want your mother to know about. The bank, the banker, and the house at Lookout Point were all a front for that. Take it with a grain of something, but that's what I've been told all my life.

When the banks went bust, the banker left town and the mansion was abandoned. In the mid-thirties, my uncle was paid by the state to live there and watch the place and see that no one came back and carted anything away.

Now it was just a one-story pile of rubble with a three-story fireplace overlooking the river, the lake, and the surrounding countryside. Not far from there, going up river, was the Belle Starr overhang. Going down river was the cave, our reason for being there. (Or so we thought).

The cave was part of the folklore that went with the house at Lookout Point. That's where they hid their booty, mostly moonshine whiskey. When the house was abandoned and the dam gave way, emptying the lake, this entire area lost its tourist appeal. The cabins emptied out. Scrubs grew into trees, bushes became impenetrable, and the cave just disappeared. No one had seen or visited it in over twenty years. Until the three of us stumbled onto it a few weeks earlier.

We were camping on the river, climbing around, traversing the bluff by edging our way across tediously narrow ledges, when I spotted a flat surface below me, jutting out maybe four feet, and six feet across, large enough to stand on and catch my breath. I jumped down, felt a draft of cool air on my back, turned around, and there it was, a hole in the side of the mountain big enough to drive a car into.

We didn't get very far that first time. A little ways in, the cave turns and gets dark all of a sudden. We had no string, no candles, just a handful of matches. By a vote of two to one, we were smart enough not to try it.

*

We were better prepared this time. We each had candles. We each had matches. Donnie brought some string. Jimmy had thought to bring a flashlight, but it was in his pack, the one he threw away.

The opening was tall enough and wide enough, but thirty feet in, a cave-in blocked the way. It was an old cave-in that something or someone had tunneled through to get in. Or out. It was necessary to crawl on your hands and knees for a ways. Then it opened into a small chamber, cold as an icehouse, its walls made of limestone, wet and slimy.

We took turns leading the way. Mostly the passage was long and narrow, with a stable floor. But you had to watch for pitfalls, some as much as a foot or two deep, some filled with water so clear and eerily still, you couldn't tell if it was a few inches deep or a few feet. Donnie and I tried to work our way around the pools, but Jimmy waded right in.

The main tunnel was not more than five feet high and three or four feet wide. But there were crevices going off in all directions rippling through the mountain to god knows where, animal dens perhaps — there were still a few cougar around, and plenty of bobcat. Some of the crevices were almost wide enough to be tempting, but not quite. We stayed to the main channel, entranced by the spectacle of stalactites and stalagmites, some of them looking like frozen waterfalls. The movement of shadows caused by the candles made it feel like we were being watched by something or someone. We were unusually quiet, all three of us — a kind of religious quiet, made of equal parts awe and fear.

By the time we reached the 'main room,' we'd run out of string and gone through half our candles.

The main room was thirty feet long, and half that wide, with a high ceiling. The floor seemed to have a soft and uniform consistency. It dawned on all of us at the same time: Bat guano! In that same instant, we recognized the commotion starting up overhead as the entire ceiling came alive. We screamed in unison and flattened out on the floor of the cave, our faces buried in our arms, while every bat in the world flapped and screeched its way to the back of the cave, then, moments later came back through on the way out.

That broke the tension. We sat in the dark and laughed until we were almost sick. Sitting on a mountain of bat shit, we ate the last of our Peanut Butter Logs, shared another bologna sandwich, and moved on.

Shortly after we left the main room, we came up against the first obstacle that caused us to consider turning back: another cave-in, old and well-trampled, but exiting into a small, dark hole which angled steeply down, and seemed to have no bottom. We tossed a stone in and listened to it bounce a few times and then hit water, maybe eight or ten feet below. But there was no way of telling how deep the water was, or what else might be down there. As Donnie and I saw it, we had but two choices.

We could quit right there and go back.

Or we could tie a rope around Jimmy's waist and lower him into the hole.

Head first, and with a candle in each hand, we slowly lowered Jimmy into we didn't know what. He grumbled and fussed all the way down.

It turned out to be just another tunnel like the one we were in, and filled with ankle deep water. But getting there required squeezing through a space too narrow to maneuver in or see what lay below, and a three-foot blind drop at the bottom.

From there, it was a short distance to the back of the cave. It ended in a small room, startling in its finality, and unlike anything we'd seen so far. The room was almost perfectly round, maybe ten feet in diameter, and dry, no cracks, no crevices, no leaks — like one huge boulder had been chiseled out and removed to create the space. There was a busted keg, two tin cups, and a bean can. There was a fire-pit in the middle, and the remnants of a fire. We had one candle left between the three of us.

We blew out the candle and sat for a few minutes in absolute dark, listening to our own breathing. Again, I felt like we were being watched — actually felt something touch my face and pass lightly through my hair. We all felt it. But no one said anything at the time, not a word until we were out of the cave and up on top, making camp for the night.

That's when we realized we'd shared approximately the same sensation. I suspected Prune but didn't say anything. What could I say? (I mean, I couldn't very well tell them it was just Prune exploring his brain like it was a cave, indeed he was exploring my brain and their brains, all of us, and for *what?* What did he hope to find? A key, a protean maya, some secret for unlocking Mother Nature's closet where he just knew she was hiding all her nasty panties? Could I tell them that? And could I tell them he'd already found that key a number of times, and that each time, it looked like the key, it felt, smelt, and was shaped exactly like the key, but it didn't fit into anything? Huh, could I tell them that? Of course not. I didn't know it myself. So I didn't say anything.)

Getting out was easy. We only had one candle, but we knew the way. We were noisy and careless — I want to say fearless, but that's not exactly true. As the last of our candle died, we broke out of the cave, spattered with candle grease, covered with mud, and worn out. There was just enough daylight left to scramble up the bluff and find a place to camp for the night.

We followed Donnie to a place he seemed familiar with, a place some woman or other had taken him to, he said.

He led us straight to the circular clearing in the woods where Belle brought me to dance. There was the bluff overlooking the river on one side of the circle, and the big round boulder on the other. I'd never been there without Belle, never been able to find it on my own. I felt both surprised and a little betrayed, though I don't know why exactly. And I got over it.

By my calculations, we were directly above the cave.

*

The night was warm and clear but we built a fire anyway. It had been an exhausting two days and nights. Jimmy and Donnie fell asleep immediately. I watched the fire burn down, ate a piece of bread, drank water from my canteen, slept for awhile without dreaming, and woke up with a start, feeling like I'd fallen to earth from someplace high and far away. Clouds were forming in a corner of the sky, with heat lightning, but no hint of rain. I watched what I thought to be the moon; watched it move away from the clouds then fall sharply out of sight. I heard a loon nearby, warning me about something.

Between strokes of lightning, I woke up again, and two men were standing beside the fire. They were men and they were not men. I mean, they cast no shadow, and seemed to move in their own light. The light was soft and kind, and when the two men smiled, I could see that they were the same man — same hair, same features, same person except that one was older and taller than the other. One was about my age and looked like Donnie. The other man, the older one, wasn't really old but he wasn't a kid either. He was a young man and that was Donnie too. The younger man stepped up to the older man, then into the older man, and became him.

We were joined by someone who looked like Grandma Belle as a young woman. She had long dark hair, black eyes and a beautiful face, and descended on us like snow, like flakes of light that became Belle as they touched the ground. I wanted to go to her but couldn't for some reason. She said something to Donnie and they both laughed.

He picked her up in his arms and began walking, and all at once they were far away already; they walked up to the boulder at the edge of the clearing, stepped inside it, and disappeared. I looked around at the clearing; it was big and empty; I was alone and nothing cared about me. I felt devastated. I wept for what seemed like a long time. And then I woke up again.

The sun was coming up and Jimmy was beginning to stir. Donnie was smiling at the edge of his sleep. He looked pleased, and woke up chuckling. Then his face went sober and I could see him thinking about something. I saw a little girl, he said. She had long dark hair and black eyes. Then he smiled again, and said, I used to be her pony.

He got up, stretched, and walked straight to the round boulder. He walked all the way around it, as though he had not seen it before. Then he pissed into the bushes and made himself a bologna sandwich.

Jimmy said, I hope I never see another goddam bologna sandwich in my life. And finished off the last of it.

Then we went home.

Ten years later and hundreds of miles apart, Donnie and Belle died within minutes of each other. I was in jail in Tucson, Arizona when first one called to me, then the other. I was sick myself, but did what I could for each of them, what I knew to do.

Then I fell asleep, dreamed, and woke up, sort of, recalling the events detailed above, pretty much the way you see them.

*

Without Guardrails
{^}

The first time I saw Jenny Lynn was a transcendent experience from which I have never fully recovered.

We were nine years old, in the third grade, and she had just moved to Siloam from some city so big and far away I couldn't even imagine it. It was in the middle of the day, in the middle of a class period, and I had stepped into the hall on my way to the coatroom for I don't remember what. And there she was, coming out of the classroom across the hall, doing the same thing for the same reason. I'd heard there was a new girl. I knew everyone in school and she wasn't one of them, so it had to be her — a tiny little thing, petite, with honey-blond hair that hung to her waist, and features so perfectly formed that she seemed older than the rest of us, more mature.

We stepped into the hall and seemed to see each other at the same time. Nothing before or since could have prepared me for what happened next.

In the instant that I saw her, she seemed to turn into a woman — granted, a very small woman, but a woman nonetheless — and wearing a wedding gown, *sixteen* wedding gowns to be exact, all the same woman wearing sixteen different wedding gowns from sixteen different periods in history — *pre*history even. All of this in the time it takes to glance at each other and look away. I didn't know what to say or do, so I did neither. She went into the coatroom and disappeared.

I don't know what all that means, exactly. I have my suspicions. But this is not a book of suspicions, so we'll leave it alone for now.

After that initial sighting, I couldn't wait for recess. Every recess. I tracked her down and followed her, but from a distance. I was too shy to speak to her, but she knew I was there. She passed furtive little glances in my direction, and allowed herself to be stalked.

We began to flirt, sort of. I mean, while we didn't speak to each other directly, both of us became more animated and vocal when speaking to anyone else within sight or hearing of the other. This went on for weeks. But not until Valentine's Day did everything come out in the open.

On Valentine's Day, the entire school was allowed to have a party and exchange valentines. I had twenty cards for twenty kids, and one for my teacher. But I had five extra cards, each hand picked and personal, ranging in sentiment from that of a child to something an adult might give to a lover. At recess, I snuck up on Jenny, stuck the cards in her hand, and took off running. I didn't stop running till I got home, and didn't go back to school that day or all of the next.

(Prune sent her a card too. He wrote something long and involved but wouldn't let me read it. To this day I don't know what it said or if she ever received it.)

*

Jenny lived four miles out of town at a place called Possum Valley Ranch, although I don't recall ever having seen a possum near there. Nor was it much of a ranch. It looked like a postcard of what a ranch should look like. Sitting in a narrow valley between two ridges of wooded hills, it had a rock house and a barn (I want to say red, but it was white), and a few rows of garden vegetables. There was a creek that cut across the yard, with a wooden footbridge over it, a pond beyond that. Inaccessible to farm stock, the pond was put there for its own sake. Manicured and stocked with fish, it was a lily pond, I guess. It had a dock and a rowboat. At the narrow end of the valley was a log cabin where my Uncle Lacey once lived as a young man.

On sunny afternoons, I used to make a lunch and hike the four miles out to Possum Valley with Smokey at my heels. Once there, we'd climb up the hill across the road and above the house, and wait for Jenny to show herself. Sometimes she did, but not often. She never knew we were there. After an hour or so, I'd share my lunch with Smokey, and the two of us would make the long walk back to town. Once, I made the mistake of taking Jimmy with me.

My Aunt Polly made sandwiches for us both, wrapped them in a kerchief and tied that to a hobo pole. By the time we got to the ranch, Jimmy was hot and tired. He'd eaten both his sandwiches, and was devising some sort of attack plan. He couldn't see why we didn't just go down and knock on the goddam door. I didn't have a good explanation, other than that just wasn't what I had in mind. So we fought about it. I had to sit on his head to keep him from yelling out. Then it began to rain, hard. We walked back to town in the rain, tried to hitchhike but looked too much like something drowned and washed up by the river. Jimmy never stopped bitching the whole way.

*

I never got over being shy around Jenny. I stammered and stumbled, sounded generally foolish. I couldn't have a conversation with her without having flashbacks of her in one of those wedding gowns, or something equally bizarre. Once she was the princess of something and I was a priest — our love got me banished from the kingdom. The next day she was a temple prostitute and I was a member of the royal family. Another time we appeared to be a pair stepped right out of a bible story. Stuff like that. We had lives together in France and Italy, more than one in Egypt, Atlantis, and Peru, recently in New York, and another in Eureka Springs, not far from where this one is taking place. Of course, at that time I had no idea what was going on; I'd never heard of reincarnation or past-lives or anything of a sort. I just knew that each time I saw her she was someone different, and I fell in love with her all over again.

I visited her in dreams much the same way Donnie and I visited each other, but unlike Donnie, she never seemed to remember them when she woke up. I have spent an inordinate amount of my adult life searching out the places we visited in dreams, the two of us zipping around the astral world, hiking in the Himalayas, swimming naked in the Mediterranean, having a picnic at Machu Pichu. Our spirits were close, almost the same thing, even our physical proximity was not so far apart. But we might as well have been living on different planets. Her ego had things to do and learn in order to bring her own soul into balance. My ego had its own agenda for much the same reason. But it wouldn't work and I knew it. I would never be anything but Billy Mack to her, while she would be all she is to me. (And that would have been unbearable.)

After that initial surge, she didn't give me much to go on, no real encouragement. I wanted to hear the words. But she never said them. Once, after I'd moved to Tulsa, she wrote them in a letter: *I love you.* My mother died not long ago, and left behind a trunk filled with old photos, news clippings and such, among them, a dozen letters from Jenny to me, written over forty years ago.

Once, Prune, aware of my dilemma, tried to help by teaching me to play multi-dimensional chess with time, a game in which present, past, and future run parallel and simultaneous to one another. The idea was for me to choose my destiny by undoing the past and re-ordering the future with some powerful and emotive action in the present. I drove over to Siloam with the idea of presenting this possibility to Jenny. But she was locked into a fixed situation that I couldn't alter without creating problems I had no right to impose just to satisfy my own desires. Her mind couldn't and wasn't really interested in making such a leap into the unknown at that time, so I didn't even bring it up.

We have gone on to marry other people, have children, families, good lives, if difficult sometimes. The last time I saw her she was still preoccupied with perhaps the only person I have ever met for whom I have no earthly use — a marriage arranged for *this* lifetime while in *another*. Go figure.

And there's this, perhaps the longest journey taken in a split second, from then to now, without pause: in the barn with Jenny Lynn, wearing a gold scarf, her honey-colored hair almost to her waist. We were looking for a rope to toss over the rafters and tie her hands above her head. It was my idea, but she's the one found the rope and showed me how to tie it. We were twelve years old. I was supposed to tie her up and kiss her, but I couldn't. I was afraid I wouldn't know how. Or when to stop. For forty years I have ached for what I did not dare to do. And have spent most of my life since, living in a world without guardrails, willing always to take a chance.

*

Losing A Friend
{^}

Not long after the flood, my best friend at the time got run over by a train, sort of, thrown from a bridge trestle into the waters of Sager Creek and swept a mile downstream. It was a life-changing experience for my friend, and I know it to be true because I was there. I saw the whole thing.

We'd gone down to the railroad bridge after school to check out the flood waters and ogle a magazine that belonged to his uncle. It was a magazine full of naked women in odd postures. The color foldout was especially startling. So much so, that when we decided to climb up the underside of the bridge he took the foldout with him.

A passenger train came through every afternoon on its way to Kansas City, and we knew it. But when the whistle blew at the half-mile intersection, we both got a rush of adrenalin. I nearly climbed down right there. But my friend tucked the magazine into his pants and climbed higher, all the way to the top, just below the tracks. He stuck his hand between the crossties and wiggled his fingers then pulled it back. Scary stuff. When the engine rumbled onto the end of the bridge I screamed and hung on, but my friend already had his pants down to his ankles and was involved in what we both knew was a sin.

If the arrival of the train hadn't coincided so perfectly with his actions, my friend might have gone on to live an almost normal life. But when the train hit the bridge at full throttle his attention was elsewhere and he became unmoored and fell, entangled in his trousers, into the foamy waters of Sager Creek. I watched him sail downstream, turn the bend, and disappear.

I climbed down and took off after him, past the ice plant, past Allen's Grocery, behind the Rialto Theater, Mac's Barber Shop, and the fire station, I ran, following him as he bobbed and tumbled in the water, seldom out of sight but always out of reach.

Luckily, he got caught up in the flood debris and stuck on the dam in Twin Springs Park right in the middle of town. Prune and Arlene were picnicking in the park and pulled him ashore, although she seemed inclined to let him drown. By the time I got there he was surrounded by a crowd. He was sitting up, coughing and spitting. His pants were knotted around his ankles. No one knew quite what to make of it. And my friend wasn't talking. I didn't want to talk about it either. In fact, we never did talk about it much at all. Whatever it is that makes closeness possible between people also puts them in the way of hard feelings if that closeness ends. A short time later we stopped being best friends. He went to live with an uncle in another town for a while. I saw very little of him after that, maybe six or eight times in twenty years. But I was always surprised to note how short he had gotten. I mean, he seemed to get smaller every year.

I'm not saying that he wasn't successful. He was. He was rich. He was politically well connected. He married and divorced beautiful women. It's not that his life was so *un*normal, but his person was. He didn't grow a fraction of an inch after that day under the bridge. And the more successful he got, the smaller he seemed to be. The last time I saw him he was so small he couldn't even see me. And neither one of us spoke.

*

Hitchhiking
{*}

I was eleven when I started hitchhiking. Jimmy, Donnie and I hitchhiked out Highway 33 to the bridge at Flint Creek and went swimming.

Seven miles each way, and we'd been told not to ride our bicycles on the highway. The sheriff, my uncle, told us not to go near the highway on our bicycles. Jimmy's grandmother told us not to. Donnie's mother and brother told us not to. Nobody said anything about hitchhiking..

We took turns: two of us hiding in the ditch and the third one standing beside the road with his thumb in the air, looking pitiful. The ride out that first morning was deceptively easy. It was early summer, midmorning, and our first ride, a farmer in a pickup, took us all the way. He turned off at the bridge and we got out and swam all day, jumping off the bridge, diving off the dam, sunning ourselves and sliding on the flat rocks below the falls. By late afternoon we were exhausted, hungry, sunburned, and ready to go home. Seven miles.

It was after dark, after dinner, and a half dozen rides later before we finally got back to town. I was staying at my Aunt Juliet's and still had two miles to walk.

On the way, I got swimmy-headed and lay down in a grassy ditch beside a meadow. I'm not sure what prompted me to lie down in the ditch, but I did. The moon and stars were out. It was a warm night. I may have closed my eyes for a moment, and when I opened them, a lens-shaped disc of light seemed to circle above the meadow, then hurtled directly toward me, pausing just a few feet above my head, so bright it was blinding. When I could see again I seemed to be in a pre-op room surrounded by beings in white smocks and surgical masks. I began to tremble and shake. I tried to scream but nothing came out. One of the beings passed a hand over my eyes and I calmed down immediately. I felt something like a finger being pressed against the center of my forehead, then a slight shock, and an electrical surge throughout my entire body. When I opened my eyes again I was alone in a ditch beneath the moon and stars, but I had the distinct feeling that someone had been standing over me only moments before, keeping watch. For just a moment my heart felt like a huge, soft ocean of light. Then I climbed out of the ditch and walked home. I wasn't hungry. I wasn't tired. I felt good, almost euphoric.

Smokey was on the front porch waiting for me, wiggling all over. Janet was mooing at me from the back gate. She didn't stop until I went around and patted her on the forehead and rubbed her ears. I led her into the barn and put her away for the night.

The house was dark. Aunt Juliet was either in the cellar or her bedroom asleep or dead or something. I drank a glass of milk and went to bed. That was on a Friday, and I didn't wake up until Sunday afternoon, forty-two hours without registering a thought or a dream, without having to get up and go to the bathroom, and with no one seeming to notice that I was not around. My forehead felt tender, slightly bruised, but I thought nothing of it at the time.

*

Later that summer Jimmy and Donnie and I stuffed our pockets full of candy bars and hitchhiked all the way to Noel, across the state line into Missouri.

    Noel is built along the Elk River at the point where Butler Creek empties into the river. You have to cross a bridge to get into town. There was a huge open air dance pavilion at one end of the bridge, with a restaurant and a bathhouse, all out in the open; you could dance right off the floor and into the river for a swim, or onto a speedboat where you could take a ride for a dollar. Colored lights were strung across the river, so it looked like Christmas all year round. The entire main street of Noel was one long arcade of candy stores and ice cream parlors and hot dog stands, even a miniature golf course. Fun stuff. Family stuff, I guess. My mom and dad used to take me there for entire weekends. It's a one hour drive to Noel from Siloam driving straight through. Jimmy and Donnie and I hitchhiked it in two. We hung out in the arcade for a while, didn't go swimming that day, and came back early, not wanting to press our luck.

    Soon after that, I began taking short trips alone and without telling anybody. I'd have this overwhelming urge to go places, undefined places that I had no previous curiosity about.

One Saturday when I was supposed to be taking a dance lesson I rode my bicycle to the edge of town, parked it behind a clump of bushes, and waited with my thumb in the air until a car stopped for me. I didn't know the man — he was a truck driver from Allen's canning factory. I got in and he asked me where I was going. It occurred to me that I didn't know. He told me his name was Frank and he was going all the way to Kansas City. You're good that far, he said.

Kansas City, I thought. I could ride all the way to Kansas City. I could get a job, do stuff, and write home about it. I told him that Kansas City would be fine. But by the time we reached Gentry, nine miles away, I lost my nerve and asked him to let me out. Then I caught a ride back to Siloam.

That was my first time hitchhiking alone. As the summer went on I ranged farther and farther away, to Gravette and Sulphur Springs and eventually to Noel by myself; once, just before the end of summer, I went as far as Van Buren. In all these towns I walked around the streets, looking in windows, waiting for something to happen, not really sure what I'd do if something did. I found myself meeting strange people who would approach me and start talking as though we were somehow familiar, or simply stare at me, knowingly, appearing to convey information into my mind, information that stayed there, locked away just out of reach. I knew that it meant something, but had no idea what. Once I thought I saw Prune disguised as a gypsy fortuneteller set up on the sidewalk in front of a store window. I've never known him to wear his hair so long and dark, nor can I remember ever having seen him in a full skirt. He was reading the cards of a man in a green suit, wearing a green tie and a badge and carrying a green case. The man wasn't sure he liked or believed what he was being told. He asked if he would soon be married, and the cards said, no, and he said aha, and asked if he would be happily married, and the cards said probably not, and he said aha, and asked what color underwear he was wearing, and the cards said he wasn't wearing any, and he said aha, and asked what color eyes he had, and the cards asked him, which one, and he said aha, and he asked what part of the world he was from, and the cards answered that on the third Wednesday of November he was closer to being here than on any other day of the year, and he said aha, and asked just what is *he* doing here, pointing at me, and Prune gathered up his cards and told the man he would never again reveal to him the truth of the cards because his green suit smelled of treachery and deceit, and the man said aha, I knew it was you, you sunuvabitch, and the two of them took off down the street in wild pursuit of one another.

Eventually I went back to the highway and stuck my thumb in the air. I was home before the end of the day. And no one missed me, ever. Now and then, Donnie would go with me, but I preferred to go alone. Alone I could be anything or anyone. I could lie. And I felt more open to chance.

By the time I was fifteen I was a veteran, staying gone for two and three days at a time without being missed. Because I lived in a small town and was related to half of it, there were any number of places I could sleep at night and no one worried about me. If I didn't show up where I was expected, it was assumed that I was sleeping at a relative's. Living with Aunt Juliet made for even less accountability. Disappearing for two and three days at a time was easy.

I was on a joyride to infinity, and the only cost seemed to be time. I kept losing time, hours, days, even weeks in which I would disappear and later be unable to explain my whereabouts. I can't tell you the number of times my mom and dad gave me what-for because I wasn't where I was supposed to be and couldn't give a good accounting for it. And when I tried to explain by being truthful —i.e., with Prune or another of my off-world visitors —I got tanned for being such an outrageous liar. I learned that living on the road was easier than living at home or staying in any one place because living on the road you don't have to explain your whereabouts, you don't even have to know yourself where your whereabouts might be.

My first extended trip was done as an afterthought. I was seventeen and living in Tulsa with my mother when I decided to hitchhike to Siloam for a few days. A friend drove me out to the highway, but on a whim, instead of going east toward Arkansas, I went west toward I didn't know where.

My first ride took me all the way to Bakersfield, California.

This, with two sisters who turned out to be a mother and her daughter — the mother couldn't have been over 32 or 33. Their first names were different, but their middle names were the same. They called each other Faye. They were on a wild ride across the country, spending 'daddy's money,' so they said. The younger of the two told me that as a very small child she was molested by a ball of light that offered her wonderful visions and voyages in return for her agreement to become a kind of messenger or something; she said she woke up in the middle of the night to find this ball of light floating around her room. It was about the size of a softball and continued to bounce off the walls until it came into contact with a beam of light coming through the window and exploded or melded or something; she said it joined with the beam of light illuminating her bed. She remembered standing up in her bed — a baby bed, actually, with bars all around; she stood up and pressed her face against the windowpane in an effort to see where the light was coming from. She followed the tube of light with her eyes, all the way back to the brightest thing in the night sky, so bright it made the stars and moon disappear. That's what she told me, her mother all the time smiling, nodding her head, watching the road. Taking turns driving, we drove straight through from Tulsa to Las Vegas where they put me up for the night, for *three* nights, the three of us sharing a suite. Faye and Faye taught me things in those three days I am still trying to forget.

At Bakersfield they went north and I turned around and headed home. I was nervous, kinda, not sure how long I'd been gone but not in any real hurry. This was before the Interstate Highway system, on old Highway 66, which passed through the middle of every town along the way. I dawdled in Barstow and Needles and Kingman, kept running into people who'd been 'abducted' by the light and the *beings* who live in it. I wasn't sure if there were really that many of us, or were we made to somehow seek each other out. I was beginning to wonder if the earth wasn't just some giant transit lounge where entities from other worlds do business — sometimes in their own bodies, sometimes by inhabiting ours. That's what I thought, but I had no idea what it meant. At Williams, Arizona I thought about taking a side trip to see the Grand Canyon, but decided to save that for another time. This was, after all, a trial run. I was almost three weeks getting back to Tulsa. All this, while my mother thought I was in Siloam staying with relatives who didn't have a clue. I might have gotten away with it had I not landed in jail in New Mexico for expectorating on a policeman's shoe. Twice. Once by accident, and again after being thumped on the head and told not to. Listen: I was just hitchhiking through, minding my own goddam business, when three locals drove by in a pickup truck and hit me in the chest with a beer bottle, then drove around the block and tried to do it again, but missed, and I heaved the first bottle through their rear window. A fight ensued, costly to all concerned, but a joy, a real joy, that ended with me spitting blood on a policeman's foot and being arrested — not for assault and battery, not for being a public nuisance, but for 'flaunting the law'. All of it a precursor of things to come.

*

Janet
{^}

The first children who saw the big, brown and white body floating on the stock pond let themselves think it was a sea monster. But it didn't act like a monster, and it had a beautiful face. By the time all the children in the neighborhood had gathered at the pond, word had gotten around that it was Janet. Everybody knew Janet.

Once they got over the initial shock, some of the older boys started throwing rocks and sticks at her. Coming down the road on my way home from school, I heard Smokey barking and saw the crowd of kids in our pasture. I went running and only then did I realize what had happened.

I bounced a rock off the oldest of the boys, and slammed headlong into the back of another, sending him sprawling face down in the mud and ooze at the edge of the pond. I screamed something — I don't know what. I picked up a dead tree limb and began swinging it at anyone who got near Janet or me. I was crazy, capable of murder, and everyone knew it. Even the Malveccio boys, older, bigger, tougher than me, knew it. I continued to scream and throw mud and rocks until everyone backed away, well out of reach, all of them standing in a hushed cluster a good distance from the pond. I sat down in the mud, sobbing. Smokey sat down in the mud beside me. Something in my thirteen-year-old heart broke and would not stop breaking.

I sat in the mud until after dark. By then everyone had given up being curious or concerned and gone home. I lay down in the tall grass not far from where Janet floated on the water, and Smokey lay down beside me.

In the night I heard my Aunt Polly and Uncle Gark calling to me, asking if I was out there, and was I all right. My aunt put a blanket over me and Smokey, while my uncle lit a smudge pot and put it in the mud close to Janet, said that would keep animals away until he could come back in the morning with a winch.

I cried until I fell asleep, and only then did I notice a yellow flicker, a dot of light in the corner of my eye. I seemed to unhinge my consciousness from my body and crawl to the dot of light which turned out to be a miniature tunnel at the end of which I could see mountains and streams and stars and wind and rain and sheets of emotion looking like colored streams of light; I saw a milky pool and what appeared to be angels — gods and goddesses, demons and deities alike — all drinking from the milky pool, the pool itself, formed by a stream of light pouring from my heart.

After that, all manner of creatures came to drink at the pool, mammals I'd never heard of, birds I'd never seen, snakes eating themselves and shedding themselves and eating themselves. And Prune was there. He seemed to be everywhere, taking care of Janet, taking care of Smokey, seeing to it that I didn't die of a broken heart. I could have. I wanted to. I came awake and the moon had settled comfortably on the ground.

I woke up beside Smokey and Janet, staring into the burning smudge pot. For a moment there was no skin on earth I could not put on, no plant or animal, no man or woman I could not enter and become.

Don't ask me what that means. At the time I seemed to know, but not anymore. I don't remember what happened after that either. I could invent something, but the truth is, I don't remember anything about the next morning or my uncle returning with the winch. I have effectively blocked all that out. Janet was gone. There was nothing I could do for her, yet she had altered my whole universe.

I feel now pretty much the way I did then, that the dead should not be taken so abruptly; instead, they should just trail gradually off in the distance so that we can still see them on the hill or across the river, in our dreams perhaps, from which we awaken healed and almost new, hearing them tell us not to worry, it's all right to be dead, we're used to it already. How they go is never the way we want or expect them to.

Not long after that, my Aunt Juliet went into the hospital and never came out. And not long after that I was told that Smokey followed a booger into the woods and just kept on going. By then I was packed and ready to move again.

*

The Circus
{^}

Every year I tried to run away from home and join the circus.

I'd dress up like a dancing bear by putting on a hat and shoes and clothes that buttoned up the front. Then I'd go to the circus and parade around on two feet, eating everything offered me — nuts, popcorn, licorice sticks, balls of cotton candy. All that while applying for work at every sideshow booth up and down the midway. The only person who even considered hiring me was Bob, 'the animal man.' Bob was responsible for the care and feeding of all the animals in the circus: the lions and tigers and bears and weasels, a dozen or so trick dogs, and the occasional elephant. The first time I got hired on, there were two elephants, and my job was to fetch water and shovel-up after them. It paid two dollars a week.

On the second day, I paid Donnie one dollar to finish out the week for me. Two days later, Donnie had Jimmy doing all the shoveling, just for the 'privilege. ' To hear Jimmy tell it, he was an apprentice animal trainer.

The circus came to town for one week every year just before Labor Day. It was a one-ring circus, one big tent and a bunch of sideshows exhibiting the wonders of the thin man, the fat lady, a two-headed baby in a jar, and a hula dancer with a really interesting tattoo. Not much I'm afraid. But it was a big deal to me, laid out as it was, on the fairgrounds at the edge of town.

I was expected to arrive early enough to water the elephants and shovel-up whatever mischief they'd done in the night, before the midway filled with people. Bob didn't want paying customers tracking elephant doodoo everywhere. So that first day, my last as it turned out, I was up at dawn.

Actually, I'd been up most of the night, anticipating something without knowing what. This was the last week of summer vacation, hot and sticky, the nights muggy and still. The fairgrounds was just an empty pasture that stretched for a couple hundred yards along Sager Creek. I dawdled down the path, wired but tired and ringing wet by the time I reached the creek where I thought to start the day off by dangling my feet in the water. I took off my shoes. The cool water sent chicken skin up and down my body. Then I took off my pants, my shirt and all. It was early in the morning. I was hidden by weeds and trees and a steep bank on both sides. I thought I was alone. Until a pair of women's underwear floated by, and soap suds. Then I heard splashing upstream and around a bend in the creek.

Careful not to make a ripple or a noise, I made my way upstream, hiding in the marshy weeds, my body submerged. Then I saw her. A woman from the circus, I guess. Full-bodied but not fat, about thirty, which seemed old to me at the time. She was taking a bath. I saw her bob to dive, mooning me as she did so. I saw her surface and spit, then shake water from her hair. I saw her breasts, watched her lift them with her hands then let them float. I saw her wave in my direction, *holymotherofgod*, I thought I'd been caught. Half expected to be struck blind, or worse.

But she was waving at Prune hiding in the bushes above and behind me. Until that moment I hadn't noticed he was there. She must've startled him because he tried to escape by turning into something, but before he could decide what, she called to him.

Now I'd been warned all my life to beware of the ill-born wench who can make the tenderest vegetables wither with just a touch, can even make mold grow on fresh bread and gold turn black. I wondered if she was that sort of wench. I hoped not. Prune was doomed if she was.

Come here, she said to Prune, let me show you something. He hesitated, and she told him she hadn't been with a man in months. Come over here, she said again, I'll let you in on a little secret, might even share it with you.

I'm not sure if what Prune felt was fear or religious awe, but he was trembling like a leaf, more frightened, more alone, more not knowing what to do than either of us could remember, so he did as he was told. Just look at you, she said, and gathered him into her bosom filled with pity and a mother's love, then she took him by the hand and guided him into her body because he couldn't seem to manage alone and afraid and confused by panic and not knowing where things went exactly, she indicated to him with a mother's voice to get a good grip on her shoulders so the current wouldn't knock him over, and not to squat down in the water but to kneel firmly on the bottom breathing slowly so he'd have enough wind, and he did as he was told. I was wondering, why is it women do things as though they were inventing them.

But it was all new to Prune. She told him to *wait!* And that, he couldn't do.

She laughed and patted him on the head. Poor baby, she said. You'll do better next time. I'm sure of it. Then she climbed out of the water and wrapped herself in a big flowerdy towel. I watched her walk across the fairgrounds even as the circus was beginning to stretch and yawn and come awake. When I looked back Prune had vaporized, gone.

I wasn't sure what I'd witnessed, or how I felt about it. Weak and queasy for sure, I tingled all over. And I kinda wanted to die — just close my eyes and when I opened them be someone else somewhere else. I floated around for a few minutes feeling guilty, ashamed, embarrassed, and sort of proud of myself for no reason. I wondered about the secret, what it was exactly, and was any of it left? Then I swam back to where my clothes were, still looking around for Prune. But he was nowhere in sight. (In fact, I wouldn't see him again until the night after the fair closed and the circus left town.)

By the time I got to work the elephants had already made enough water to cause the whole midway to smell like ammonia. I spread sawdust and shoveled manure all morning. And did my best to be invisible — didn't ride the rides, didn't walk the midway, didn't play the milk bottle game or smash up kewpie-doll plates, I refused to make eye contact with anyone, hoping to avoid the lady from the creek. That afternoon I found Donnie and sold him my job for a dollar. He was better suited for the circus life than me anyway, much better suited.

*

Two days later a cold wind came up and it started to rain.

It rained day and night, causing the creek to jump its banks and the circus to leave town a day early. That was fine with me. I had decided to avoid the circus for the rest of the week and not risk running into the naked lady. In spite of what I'd seen, I still considered myself a virgin. But I didn't want to tempt fate any more than fate had already been tempted. So I didn't go near the creek or the fair grounds till the circus was done and gone, and even then it wasn't something I chose to do. It happened like this:

The day after the circus left, I woke up sometime in the night. A dog was barking outside my window. I got up to see what all the commotion was about and when I stepped out the back door I seemed to come awake in someone else's dream. I was in someone's pasture beneath an enormous and brilliant moon. I remember thinking that this was not our pasture, we don't have a pasture, don't even live near one. My second thought was that this wasn't a pasture at all, but the empty fairgrounds. I was standing in the middle of the fairgrounds, miles from home, still in my nightgown, and I knew immediately that it was not a dream. I was where I thought I was, and had no idea how I'd gotten there. I was terrified — almost beyond terror because it had no name. My heart was pounding and my nightgown was soaked with sweat and sticking to my freezing skin. I had chewed my lip bloody.

After a week of rain, the sky was suddenly full of stars, more stars than I'd ever seen, all bearing down on me with a deafening humm, some of them zipping around like fireflies, others like flying footballs of light; one, larger than all the others, seemed to fall right out of the sky on top of me, slowly and steadily, growing larger as it fell, until it swallowed up every other star, moon and planet in the heavens, the whole night sky became one giant bowl of light orbiting above me. I stood there for a long time, unable to move. Off in the distance I thought I saw my house, or at least the house I had just come from. At the same time, I knew it wasn't possible to see my house from where I stood. And it wasn't my house either. Yes, it was where I'd been sleeping and where my mother was sleeping now. But it wasn't my home. For a moment I felt like I had abandoned my home to come here, to planet Earth. I didn't cry and I didn't scream.

I stood utterly still and waited, because I knew if I waited long enough, the terror would find a source and a name. Once it had a name, no matter how awful, I would be able to live with it. I could go back home, wherever that is.

Eventually the terror gave way to awe, and that, to curiosity. The curiosity then shaped itself into a huge bus. Even now, I can see it: It is a yellow school bus, and it's parked in the middle of the pasture, waiting. I am waiting too, while loads and loads of people are being bussed in from all over the planet on these little fireflies of light. They are all being loaded into this big bus, ready to go somewhere. Prune is there with the naked lady from the creek. She and Prune seem to be laughing at something private between them. He is actually driving the bus and she is taking role, writing down names and numbers. It seems to be my job to 'hold the space' while each person cleans and clears his soul pattern (I would not understand that one for another twenty years.) Once that is done and everyone is on board, I walk over and touch the bus with some device in the palm of my hand, not really sure what. But the moment contact is made the whole bus disappears in front of my eyes. No explosion, no sound, nothing. It's just gone. I have mixed feelings, at once terrified and saddened by the loss, but glad to have done it. Then I head for home, and start off on a dead run across the pasture toward the lights of the city. I'm wondering how I'll get across the swollen creek, and why they — whoever *they* is — couldn't just drop me off where they picked me up in the first place, instead of taking me clear across town and dumping me in the empty fairgrounds..

Now I'd had flying dreams and visitation dreams and incidents of lost time all my life. But never anything like this. I was aware that I had crossed some sort of line over which I was unable to cross back. My life would never again be the same.

I had to walk an extra mile to get around the creek and back to where I had gone to sleep several hours before. Dirty, tired, and chilled to the bone, I tore my sweaty nightshirt off, tossed it in the corner, and crawled into bed just moments before the alarm went off and my mother called to me to get up, it's the first day of school and you don't want to be late. Then she came into the room and turned on the light, picked up my nightshirt, looked at it, looked at me, and left without a word. Already I could smell toast from the oven, and boiling hot chocolate.

*

Mothers, Lovers, Angels, and Ugly Women
{^}

Among humans, my mother was always my favorite person --- kinda cool, not too hip, intelligent and friendly. Everyone loved her. She was a beautician and would talk to anyone, anywhere, in grocery stores or ticket lines or restaurants, drawing them out and listening to their stories with quiet compassion and curiosity. My mother made the world feel friendly and safe, even when it was neither.

She even listened to my stories without being critical. Of course, she never really knew what to do with my other-world visitors (can't call them 'playmates' — we seemed to always be doing serious stuff). Whenever I brought them up her eyes sort of glazed over and she stopped talking altogether. After awhile I learned to keep most of that to myself.

Thinking of my mother now, two memories come to mind, and a dream — with a bit of Prune's mother thrown in.

My mother and I lived in a barn-shaped house on the hill above Siloam Springs less than a mile from the center of town where my mother's beauty shop was, between the pool hall and Carl's Chevrolet. (I was actually born above the pool hall, but that's another story; you've heard most of it.) On evenings when my mother was late getting off work, I'd ride my bike down to meet her. We took long walks around town, making plans, eating burgers at Nora's Café, or just window shopping, pausing in front of store windows to consider our next purchase. We always shopped for things that were perfectly useless or more than we could afford. After a few turns around town, we cut through the park, across the dam, up the steep path, and into the neighborhood where we lived.

Once in the neighborhood, our considerations changed. We shopped for houses. Big, pretentious houses. Houses with huge porches and sculpted yards. Houses that already had dogs and someone else's children playing with them. Then we went to our rooms in the barn-shaped house where I did my homework and read comic books, and the two of us listened to Red Skelton and Baby Snooks on the radio.

We had three rooms strung together like a tunnel or a train car. But they were clean and white. Too white. The walls, the ceiling, beds, coffee table, chest of drawers, kitchen cabinets, every stick of furniture was painted an industrial strength white. It made your eyes hurt sometimes. But it made everything seem, if not new, at least clean. And that made my mother happy.

In this particular memory, the town has new streetlights, tall, arching things that make an inverted bowl of light over the city. It is November, the first snow. My mother and I are standing at the curb, waiting for the light to change. Because of the snowstorm the streets are almost empty. There is wind and snow in our faces, but we don't mind. It's just raw enough for us to take note and laugh about it. Actually, we both like the snow, so it's more exhilarating than a bother. My mother looks young and pretty tonight. She is in her early thirties and has already met her third husband. But I don't know that yet. My dad has been gone for some time, and my mother and I have been living alone, taking care of each other. She's been worried lately; it has started to show in her face. But not tonight. Tonight she just seems soft, light and buoyant about something. It occurs to me that I don't know what that something is, but it seems to have little to do with me. I have just asked her if she thinks it's possible for us to go on loving someone after we are dead. She is quiet, thoughtful, but not glazed over. Suddenly, for the first time in our singular life together, it dawns on me that she might need more than me. Nothing she says, exactly. Nothing she does. But something causes me to think I just might not be enough.

And I'm all right with that. Everything is all right. We're going to be just fine.

That night she made us hot chocolate and toast, buttered, covered with sugar and cinnamon, and toasted in the oven.

*

A few weeks later, my mother went to dinner with someone and came home late, stumbling, humming to herself.

I never slept well when my mother was out, so I was still awake when she came in. I listened to her fumble with her keys, listened to the door open and close. She stood just inside for a moment, then crossed the room and sat down on her bed. She was crying or giggling, I couldn't be sure. "Mom?" I said. When she didn't answer I got up and went over to her. "Are you okay, Mom?" She looked away and didn't say anything, but a shudder went all through her and into me. I put my arms around her. She was sobbing gently.

I rocked her and hummed something, probably religious. I was practiced at this and felt good doing it, not because she needed it, but because I needed it. I hoped she was crying because she missed my dad. But I knew better. In fact, now I know that part of her crying was because she didn't miss him at all.

She exhausted herself, and I helped her into bed. She became giddy, laughing and making fun of herself, said I reminded her of her mother — my grandmother, the religious icon who died in the pulpit, literally, dropped in the middle of a tent revival when some kid playing outside the tent tossed a rock and it skipped under the raised tent flaps and, freakishly, ominously, hit my grandmother in the temple, felling her on the spot. That wasn't what my mother was remembering when she told me I reminded her of my grandmother, but it is what comes to mind now, at the occasion of this telling. And she didn't let go of my hand until she fell asleep.

In that moment, I felt like I could be dropped anywhere in any weather, just as I was, and in no time improvise a shelter, kindle a fire, and snare an animal for dinner. My mother could do that to you, cause you to expand and become more.

*

In writing this, I am reminded of my mother's passing twenty-odd years later. It was the very day I met Prune's mother, I think. By that I mean I met someone, just not sure who. Or what. It was a jangled day, filled with mixed signals and conflicting emotions. Bear with me here:

I believe I told you that Prune's mom was an unnatural woman? Truth is, her whole *being* was unnatural. She was a saint, a true expression of the Divine Mother, though not necessarily the virgin kind.

Listen: I'd always imagined God to be some better human personality enthroned in a distant place, a sort of cosmic autocrat who ran a splendid though flawed show in which human beings were the clowns or, more precisely, the gladiators who always lost. I've only recently begun to accept the possibility that God is, in fact...*everything*. That said, I have to consider God's feminine side: God as the Divine Mother. I liked my mother, but it is boggling. And Prune's mother? Well...

Like all charismatic figures, there is no end the Divine Mother cannot and will not go, in order to excite the religious imagination. Indeed, in Her efforts to bring balance and comfort to humanity, She has taken on a host of untoward incarnations, assuming the local customs and costumes as well. In so doing, the human incarnation of this most holiest of spirits cannot be so very different from other human beings. God, in Her all-knowing imagination, created us all, and then entered in.

Prune's mom was one of the Divine Mother's more interesting incarnations; one in which she was known to have assumed the most repulsive disguises, just to test the blind faith of men she made love to.

This was in the Boston Mountains, at the edge of the Ozarks and just down from Mount Gayler. She was known as the Angel of Shaeburg Hollow. Thanks to her, no woman in that corner of the Ozarks ever need suffer sexual frustration; for, be she ugly, deformed, senile, or pubescent, she has only to knock on any stranger's door with a request for sexual favor/relief, to be welcomed by the men as if she were the most beautiful woman on earth.

Nor does the woman of the house object if she asks to make love to that woman's husband, father, or son. On the contrary, the woman of the house can hardly keep her delight within the limits of decorum, so thrilled is she at the thought that the visitor might possibly be Angel, the Divine Mother in disguise.

The day I met Prune's mother, I was sitting out a snowstorm in Buffalo, Wyoming on my way to Montana. I'd been driven out of the Yellowstone by high winds and ass-deep snow. Marooned in a local tavern attached to a small hotel.

I hadn't been there half an hour when, in response to my inquiry, the barkeep nodded toward a solitary figure at the end of the bar. The 'town treasure,' he called her. She once slept with a guy who slept with a girl who slept with John Lennon. She's a tradition around here, rites of passage and all that.

She caught me looking, and before I could unlook, she approached me, smiling, her bright red lipstick all the more startling because she had no teeth.

Now, I've run hounds, swapped lies, and drunk rattlesnake piss, but I've never known what to say to a woman. Nor how to refuse them. She led me up some cold iron stairs to a room above the bar. It was the kind of room B-movie detectives wake up in, bound and gagged, hungover, beside the dead body of someone they don't know. When she undressed her body was exactly what you would imagine.

Listen: I'd been on the road for days, living on beef jerky, sleeping in the back of my van. And there was that Divine Mother thing, ya know, the Angel of Shaeburg? I couldn't be sure. I mean, I half expected a halo to appear around her head and the lines on her face to vanish and her mouth to become suddenly voluptuous; I expected to wake up any minute with someone younger, taller, prettier, someone with all their teeth; what I got was moans and groans and screams, milk pouring from her breasts, tears from her eyes, lights going off in my head as she created the world with her love-making, all of creation, every star, stone and living thing of it fanning out from the center of her...of her...I felt like I'd been mauled near to death by god Herself, making love to me in ways I couldn't begin to imagine.

But some angels are more equal than others.

And some things are exactly what they appear to be.

She was an old woman who looked like a young woman with a ravaging disease. The effect she had on men was that, after being with her, they fell more deeply in love with their own wives; they couldn't wait to get home. I felt that way myself, and I didn't have a home or a wife.

I was too old to cry, but I cried anyway. I'm apt to cry now, just thinking about it.

It stopped snowing some time in the night. By noon, the roads were open. I just wanted out of there. I stopped by to pay my bill, and peeked into the bar, thinking I might have one for the road. And there was Angel. She was sitting with a surprised looking young man who was wearing a gabardine suit and a plaid hat with a long green feather in it. She had him by one ear. "...then I spent my 6th life looking for number one, " she said, "my 7th life being co-dependent, and my 8th life doing 12 steps..." She saw me and winked.

I wondered then what I've wondered every day since: Does she know she's god? Does she know I am?

But I kept my wonderings to myself. I stepped into a crisp day in Wyoming in winter. My van groaned and labored but finally started. I filled up with gas and let some air out of the tires. Then I pulled onto the snow-covered highway. It was the very day my mother died, alone and unexpected, but it would be another three days before I got word.

*

This next is a dream that occurred on the ten-year anniversary of that snowy day in Wyoming.

I say, dream, but it's more than that. In fact, I've never had another remotely like it for lucidity and detail.

My mother and I are walking in a lush green forest when we come to a clearing with a statue in the middle. It is a black marble statue of the Buddha. In the forehead of the statue is a white spot the size of my thumb. My mother reaches out and touches the spot (was it a light? I'm not sure), and the statue splits in half, right down the middle, and the two halves fall away revealing an absolutely gorgeous baby inside — one that it seems to be my job to care for.

At the time I had no idea what any of that meant — didn't know, didn't want to know. Now I consider it to be some sort of initiation, a birth of new consciousness. It is never far from memory. And when I think of it, I feel a mother's presence all around me.

*

Thieves
{^}

By the time I was thirteen I'd been a liar and a thief for a long time, stealing change off my mother's dresser, enough for sodas and candy bars, and a nickel here, a nickel there stashed away to buy a new bicycle. But I was thirteen before I realized how much of a liar and a thief I'd become.

It started in the smoke-hole at school. Donnie and I didn't go there to smoke, but to hang out during lunch hour, watching the older boys, listening to them exchange information about women not available to the general public. It was in the smoke-hole that I bought a newspaper route from a boy who was sick of it and couldn't find any other takers. I got it for a song, almost nothing.

The idea was for Donnie and me to take care of the route together. It made thirty or forty dollars a month, money we could both use — Donnie for lunches and hair tonic, me, because I desperately wanted that new bicycle, a Schwinn I'd spotted in the window of the Western Auto Store. (I wanted that bicycle bad enough to consider stealing it. Not that I would. But I thought about it. It wasn't the sort of thought that kept me awake nights, scheming. Rather, I pictured myself riding a stolen horse across the countryside a hundred years ago, the threat of hanging always in the back of my mind.)

A week before school let out for the summer Donnie and I started delivering the *Southwest American*, a morning newspaper out of Fort Smith. We had to be at the train depot by 4:a.m.every morning. But the weather was nice, the sun came up early, so we didn't mind.

Taking opposite sides of the street, we threw papers on porches, and rocks at dogs and one another, making a general commotion. We invented war games and dreamed of doing brave, selfless deeds, generally of a military nature; dreamed the same dreams and dreamed them so elaborately that we both knew the histories of the comrades we invented together. We saw their faces, heard their voices, felt grief when our bravery wasn't enough to save them (I always ended up dying, a martyr). We finished each morning sitting on the curb eating fresh doughnuts stolen out the backdoor of the bakery.

By mid-October the nights were cooler, the mornings a bit more difficult to wake up to. Neither of us felt genuinely heroic. While it was nothing we ever discussed, I think we'd both decided to bale out at the first sign of bad weather.

It turned winter overnight.

A fine sleet was peppering the window when my alarm went off. I slipped back under the covers and considered begging off sick, letting Donnie throw the route by himself. But my mother wouldn't hear of it, thought I should be ashamed for considering such a thing in the first place.

Cold to the bone and carrying a fresh load of guilt, I made my way to Donnie's house, but when I got there he'd already devised a plan.

Donnie crossed the frozen yard and climbed into his neighbor's pickup truck. I'd never met his neighbor but I knew about him. He was a very old man, a thief himself, forced into early retirement. His truck was a piece of junk made from a bunch of other trucks, mostly Fords, some Chevys. I watched the house while Donnie hot-wired the pickup. We were new at this but it was easy, and exhilarating.

My life took on new meaning that first cold morning, driving a stolen car, eating stolen doughnuts, sneaking back and parking the truck before anyone knew we were gone. I was so pumped full of adrenaline I couldn't see, hear, or think. Afterwards, I couldn't remember the details, and those I did remember were wrong, according to Donnie. I thought we slid into a ditch and had to dig our way out. Donnie said it didn't happen. I thought we'd actually stolen the doughnuts but he insisted that the baker gave them to us. I was convinced we robbed a gas station to get gas but Donnie said we paid a dollar for it. And so on.

Ordinarily it took us about two and a half hours, but we finished the route, returned the pickup to the neighbor's driveway, and were both home in bed in less than an hour. It was just too damned easy.

So we did it again the next morning.

And the next.

We drove that old man's pickup every morning for the better part of a month, until we got stopped by the sheriff's deputy wanting to know what we were doing up at that hour, and were we old enough to be driving. Donnie was laying out a smooth story about the truck belonging to his uncle when the second deputy in the car thought he recognized me. "You're Sheriff Gammill's nephew aren't you?" "No, I'm not," I lied, at the same time Donnie was saying, "Yes, he is," thinking that would work in our favor.

And that ended whatever career aspirations we might've had for becoming car thieves. The whole episode might have come to a quiet and convenient closure right there. But it didn't.

The next day, the sheriff picked Donnie and me up after school, loaded us into the back of his squad car with the red light going around and around, and took us to see the old man whose truck we'd stolen every day for a month. The idea was to make us squirm, I guess, and Donnie was certainly doing that. The sheriff was my uncle, my dad's brother and my namesake. He was good to me, and I liked him a lot. But he had his bluff in on every other kid in town. And for good cause.

My uncle was an imposing figure, a big man with a twisted sense of humor and a volatile temper. Rumor has it that before he was sheriff he'd been an officer in the Marines, decorated and then 'tossed' for his part in an incident so outrageous that no record of it exists anywhere, no one to say what did or didn't happen, and to whom; only that he'd given orders to three men and when informed that his orders had been carried out, he promoted them and decorated them, then had them shot as common criminals because, in his words, there are orders that can be given which cannot be carried out, God damn it, anyone with common sense knows that.

To avoid scandal, my uncle was given a medal and discharged without ceremony. In the middle of the war, he came back to Siloam and got himself elected sheriff.

Whether caused by the war or something else, my uncle was damaged goods. Years later, after he'd stopped being sheriff, he would have a pain in his head that translated itself into voices so numerous and loud that he fell asleep nights with the illusion that the stars were screaming, and woke up irate, that's enough, God damn it, he shouted, it's them or me, and proceeded to shoot out every window in his house. His wife left him, and took their son. He went over to the VA hospital in Fayetteville for awhile, and when he came back, moved into the Crown Hotel across the street from the park, a stone's throw from the Community Hall and the very police station where he'd spent so many years as sheriff. He spent the rest of his years there, sleeping alone with his most feared enemy, indeed, his only enemy, his own heart.

The day they took him away for good, he got up early and dressed, and, as was his habit, walked around the corner to Gregory's Newsstand, bought himself a paper and took it back to the park and his favorite bench where he began to read — except that this particular morning all he had on was his 'dress' hat and a pair of brogans; nothing else, not even a raincoat, insisted that some sonuvabitch had stolen his clothes when he wasn't looking.

But all that was in the future, still to happen.

He pulled up in front of the old man's house, parked the squad car beside the stolen truck and we all got out. The old man (I don't remember his name) was waiting on the front porch. He looked like a lizard with a hangover, weary, solemn, older than I had imagined. He was drinking wine from a bottle and smelled slightly zoological.

As it turned out, he'd watched Donnie and me return his truck that first morning, and with more gas than it had when we left. After that, he watched us come and go every morning — no harm. We replaced whatever gas we used. My uncle, laughing at something he knew that I didn't, left me there with Donnie and that old man. Told me to wait, that he'd be back later to pick me up. I thought I was gonna be sick.

But things are never quite what they seem. True, the old man was a drunk, and he'd once been a thief, but before that, he'd been a clergyman or a deacon or some other such official in the church. It was his joining of the two vocations that caused his downfall. And he weaved a marvelous tale.

To hear him tell it, he'd spent a number of previous lifetimes as a 'man of the cloth'; had even learned to make and drink wine while living as a monk in the Rhine Valley. But that was several lifetimes ago, he said. Since then he'd been a guru in India, a preacher in Alabama, and a priest in the mountains of Peru. All true stuff, he insisted. But what he wanted more than anything, even more than being a holy man, was to be a *whole* man. And in order to balance out all those lifetimes lived honestly and responsibly, he'd chosen to spend this lifetime as a thief; a petty thief, at that.

He started his life of petty thievery at a young age. When he was a small boy his father would take him to visit his very religious aunt. She would greet him by saying, "Everything we have is yours. When you leave, please take what you need. Take this for example." And she would indicate the most valuable object in the house. Then they would all sit down and have milk and cookies.

Later, when his aunt and his father were deep in conversation, he would wander around the house until he came upon some small thing he could really use. Then he would hide the object discreetly in his pocket. In this way, he avoided embarrassing his aunt by taking less than she had offered, and he avoided embarrassing himself by discussing the petty nature of his needs.

Someone, his father or his aunt, convinced him that people with great wealth were condemned to misery because of their wealth. Horrified at the thought, and brim full of compassion, he began relieving people of the valuables that made them so unhappy.

His was a spiritual quest, an attempt to rid people of attachment to their belongings by removing their belongings. He robbed their asses. In the name of non-attachment, he took their keys, their cars, their clothes, their jewels, the family heirlooms, their hearts, the skeletons from their closets, and an occasional dark and disturbing piece of karma. That latter proved his undoing.

He had no use for what he stole. He simply removed the valuables so that they might serve some higher good aimed at enhancing the lives of his victims. He was a *holy* thief. But, he was quick to point out that you can never put aside another man's burden for him, or deprive him of his own mistakes. It'll end up costing you both.

That's what the old man said. I had no idea what he meant, but the look of contrition on his face made me a believer.

And it seems that even a little success is enough to generate cravings of ambition. After a lifetime of stealing small things in petty ways, he woke up one morning with the gnawing desire to steal the entire universe, piece by piece.

Of course storage was a problem. I mean, if you have everything, where do you put it? The trunk of his car was too small. His own room wasn't much larger. He couldn't really afford to pay all that storage. So he did the next best thing, he stored everything in his mind. Or so he said.

Donnie and I spent all afternoon on that old man's porch while he prowled through endless rooms in his mind, fondling objects of every sort and value, unburdening himself as he went, searching for a secret he promised was there, even offered to share it with us, but not now, not today, he said, come back tomorrow. He drank wine and stared into the sun's glare without blinking; we watched him swallow whole truths, bitter truths, truths which must've been like live coals burning in his heart. Seen in that light, he looked less like a lizard with a hangover than a saint with a hangover. I began to suspect that something or someone was hiding out inside that old man, someone wise and wonderfully scary, someone vaguely familiar. I just knew I was gonna be sick.

Haunted by curiosity and full of questions, I went back to the old man's house two days later but he was gone. Completely. Moved out and took the secret and his entire universe with him. The place looked like no one had lived there for years. My uncle speculated that the old man's daughter had taken him to live with her in an altered state. Missouri, I think he said. Anyway, I never saw him again. (Yeah, right.)

Not long after that, my dad came into town, grilled me for an hour on what my mother was up to, then gave me a hundred dollar bill and bought me that new bicycle. So I quit the paper route, retired and turned it over to Donnie who sold it to some new kid in the smoke-hole. By then Donnie and I were both interested in making use of the information we'd collected about women — information I found confusing then and perplexing to this day.

*

First Light
{^}

There were few conscious events or even subtle signs of otherworld activity in my life during my high school years. Hormones covered everything up, I guess. Most of the time I just thought I was losing my mind. But one night not long after I turned sixteen, a peculiar thing did happen. It happened to me in the place where I am, perhaps, most private and vulnerable. Until now, I've never admitted this to anyone.

It's like this: where girls are concerned I'm just not normal; never have been. I like them. I like them a lot, but they terrify me. And I've always felt that I lacked the peculiar talents girls look for in a male companion — the ability to dance, smoke, make small talk, and cut up in public. As an adolescent, I was so shy it was painful; it was even painful to watch, or so I'm told. So I stuck with the things I knew I could do: I played football and basketball and ran track. I made up poems, secretly. On weekends I jerked sodas at Howard Johnson's. In the three years I was in high school, I seldom went to school dances and I don't remember ever calling a girl on the telephone or asking one for a date. I went to the movies once or twice, but I don't remember who with (maybe I made it up). I wanted to do these things but didn't have the nerve. What I finally did do was far more outrageous and off-the-wall; it may even be grounds for deportation.

It was Friday night, the last week of school, and there was a dance, some end-of-the-school-year celebration at the Community Hall. I was living in Tulsa at the time, with my mother and her husband. But I felt lonely and edgy, ready to do something, not sure what. So I decided to make the two our drive over to Siloam; see what I might stir up.

The Community Hall backs up to Twin Springs Park and is built alongside the creek, just up from the dam and next door to the fire station — in those days, the police station and hospital as well, all three in one building. Setting off by itself, the Hall is a small gymnasium with a stage on one end, bathrooms on the other, a ticket window out front.

It was after dark when I arrived, warm and muggy, the dance had already started. I parked a few blocks away and walked over, coming up from the backside, along the creek. The windows of the Hall are maybe five feet off the ground, tall, un-shuttered, and without curtains. If you stay in the shadows you can see into the lighted building without being detected. You can see almost everything that goes on. I'm sure they were playing phonograph records: Elvis, Jerry Lee, Buddy Holly, all that. But all I remember was this great amorphous din of noise, and people appearing to dance to it.

Dancing isn't the only thing I can't do, but it certainly is one of them. However, I do like to watch. I like to slip into people's minds while they're dancing and go home in their head, see where they come from, what they're doing, who they're doing it to. I circled the building, careful to stay out of sight, and watched.

155

There was very little grace in the dancing. Half the people on the floor shuffled vacantly, trying to look competent and bored, while the other half seemed to be disjointed and flying apart in every direction. It looked like a sock hop in the polio ward. But there was symmetry in the dancing, and style. I mean, everyone was doing his 'own thing' but there was a right and wrong way to do it.

I continued to circle the building, furtively, peering in from the shadows. I was looking for Jimmy and Donnie but they were nowhere in sight. I recognized Coleman sitting on the edge of the dance floor surrounded by girls. He looked excited, confused, stupid and happy (a prototype for the perfect male, says my wife). To be honest, I never liked Coleman, but right then I'd have traded places with him in a heartbeat. And Prune was there, disguised as a dweeb, Girls liked him because he could dance the tail off a monkey.

The one girl I had any real interest in, the love of my life, was in the corner flirting with an older boy. She didn't know she was the love of my life. I kept my feelings secret because I believed she would find them laughable. The older boy, who I recognized and refuse to name, was trying to kiss her. I was very close to climbing through the window and slapping someone when a mixed crowd came around the back of the building laughing and cutting up. I jumped into the shadow of a huge sycamore, tripped, and nearly fell on top of someone — a girl doing approximately the same thing I was.

We leaned into each other, briefly, awkwardly, then spun away in opposite directions, apologizing as we went. I think she spoke my name but I can't be sure, and I didn't recognize her. Then she was gone. A tall, shapely thing in a full skirt, with hair pulled back and tied loosely, arms crossed under her breasts. What else she had, it was too dark to see.

I circled the building a few more times, in a mood, I guess. I'd driven two hours to get here and now I couldn't find a way in, not through the doors for sure, not through a window, though they all seemed to be open — not into all those faces and all that harsh light. Finally, I gave it up and took myself for a walk along the creek and onto the dam.

The dam itself is wide and flat on top with a narrow spillway in the middle, one you can step across or wade in, easy walking. The waters above the dam are deep and still and polluted from waste dumped upstream by the Pet Milk Plant. It's 'Posted. No Swimming Allowed'.

I stripped down to my boxers, separated the leaves floating on the surface, and eased into the water. It was oily, and not as cold as I'd expected. I remember thinking it felt like a pool of fetal liquids; wondered too, why I would think such a thing. I was shivering, but more from anticipation than anything. I was a little afraid; not sure of what, snakes perhaps, or drowning, the unknown, more so of getting caught naked. Careful to keep my mouth closed and my head above the surface, I swam a few yards out, then stopped and looked around. There seemed to be a thin violet mist hanging over the water. I could see the back of the fire station and the police station. I could see the Community Hall. I thought I felt something brush against my leg and I swam away from there fast; in doing so, I accidentally swallowed a lump of something that went down so slick I didn't even have time to gag. This wasn't working out the way I'd expected; not really sure *what* I expected. I turned and started back to the dam and was startled by what I saw.

Sitting on the dam with her feet in the water and my clothes in her lap, was the girl I'd bumped into earlier.

*

Looking back on all that happened after that, it's hard to credit my memory. I sometimes wonder if the whole business isn't some dream left hanging around until it has taken on the status of reality. But this is how I remember it:

She watched while I got out of the water, but didn't offer to give me my clothes. My boxers were wet and hardly adequate so I covered myself with leaves and my hands; we sat talking for a while. She was new in town, had finished up the semester here, had no idea how long she'd be staying. She was a couple of years older or younger than me, I can't be sure; she *seemed* older, but maybe that's because I was so socially retarded. She was fifteen going on twenty, ripe and lovely and without pretense. It was too dark to see the exact color of her hair or eyes, but she had skin so white it seemed to almost glow in the dark. And she was wearing a shawl around her shoulders, made of sheer nylon or silk, dark blue, I think, and spattered with sequins like stars.

When I asked her where she was from she told me a story about a ship that, while searching for the Holy Grail, sailed off the edge of the world and continued on forever. At particular junctions of time and timelessness, it appears again as a bright light. Shooting across the heavens, that light is chasing something that has no beginning and no end and will not stay put. She told me that she was from that ship. I said, uh huh. Then she told me that I was from there too.

I felt like I'd come awake in the middle of someone else's dream. I didn't know what to say or do. I knew if I got caught sitting there nearly naked in the middle of the park in the middle of town, things would not go good for me.

I was about to tell her how badly things could go, when she pulled the shawl up over her head and leaned into my lap, brushed the leaves and my hands away, and kissed me right on *it*. Jeesus! I thought I'd died and gone to a better place than I'd been led to believe existed. Were this to happen today, I would no doubt recognize her as an expression of the Divine Mother in one of her earthier disguises. But I was just a kid. I didn't know anything. To me, she was a disgusting, unholy heathen, *exactly* what I wanted.

She took me by the hand and led me across the dam, up the path called Lovers Lane, and into the trees. Across the creek from the Community Hall and in full view, she made a bed of leaves, fanned her skirt out, and pulled me down on top of her. *Now*, she said, directly and without guile, *put it in*.

Now, I'd kissed girls before. I'd even touched them in their private places. But this was nothing like that. I mean, kissing a girl is as much like 'putting it in' as flying in an airplane is to falling out of one. The one experience may precede the other, but it in no way prepares you for it.

I was a virgin, sort of. And I was terrified. There we were, making love on the creek bank opposite the park under the stars in front of God and everybody, and my greatest fear was that someone from the dance or the police station next door might see us. She told me not to worry, that people in the light could only see to the edge of the light; if you stay in the shadows, she said, you can see anything.

To this day I am unnerved by the implications.

*

Afterwards, I fell asleep and dreamed about every girl I'd ever known; not many — remember, I was barely sixteen and almost a virgin. Sure, I'd had sexual encounters of sorts; one comes immediately to mind and I am surprised by it, surprised by two things. One, the fact that I had forgotten or repressed it for some reason; until this writing I had no recollection whatsoever. Two, I couldn't have been over eight years old at the time it occurred; this, with a girl four or five years older. She babysat me on Saturday nights.

I had no idea what we were doing at first. She wasn't sure either, but she had a fumbling idea. We would start the evening off making popcorn and playing checkers. Then we made bubbles by blowing soap through a straw; we told stories for awhile, listened to Jack Benny and Amos 'N Andy on the radio; eventually it got to be my bedtime. But first I had to have a bath. *Ahh! Bathtime.* She was young and inexperienced but she could really give a good bath.

She started sitting with me when I was five and pretty much a child. It was her custom to prepare for bed by undressing in front of me with no thought to her nudity. It was my custom to leave my bed in the middle of the night and go to her's as a means of overcoming my fear of the dark and the weight of terrible nightmares. Contact with her seemed to alleviate both fears. Those were our customs and we continued to practice them for two or three more years, during which time I gradually became conscious of the difference in her nudity and my own. At first I noticed her breasts. I can't be sure when she became aware of them herself, but I remember the day she caught me looking too close and for too long. From that day forward, while the customs did not change, their ritual content certainly did.

One night, after all customs had been carried out, I fell asleep beside her and woke up sometime later, unable to breath. It was dark; I was anxious but not afraid; there were no nightmares present. But something in the air had settled suffocatingly around my nose and mouth and chest. Holding my breath and pretending to sleep, I felt her fingers crawl down my chest and across my stomach in search of ... *what*? I could only guess. Still pretending to sleep, I changed my position to make her search easier.

We never spoke about it, choosing to ignore what each of us knew that the other knew. I was only eight, but innately I understood this to be some sort of watermark, high or low.

We became more bold, more daring. We played goose-tag, her stripped down to her panties, me in my Fruit-of-the-Looms, the possibility of our getting caught adding to our excitement. Occasionally she'd pull her panties down and make me touch it, even put my finger in a ways. It smelled like a bait bucket. I'd wash my hand real good afterwards, but that didn't seem to help much. Nothing did. I was afraid someone would come home and want to smell my hand.

It was all a mystery to me, hardly even sexual. But she was older. Or I was younger. Something. She wanted things from me that I didn't even know existed. *Say love. Say lie down. Say touch me here. Do anything you want but don't hurt me.* She gained a reputation around town for being generous and easy to the point of extravagance. Then she went away one summer and died; barely fifteen. And I don't even remember her name.

But something in the quality of all that delivered a shock that left me unable to carry even the memory of it until this very minute, this writing.

*

I heard voices and woke up with a shiver. On the creek bank directly across from us, people were crawling around with flashlights. Someone had seen someone go into the water and not come out. Prune was in the middle of them, leading the search. He actually spotted us right off, and waved, but didn't let on to the others.

She pulled me deeper into the shadows and we watched them look for us. She pointed into the night sky at a thin sliver of light, brighter than the stars, moving slowly across the heavens. Suddenly it sped away. I was amazed. I didn't know what to think. For a brief moment I felt inconsolable and didn't know why, as if I'd lost my very best friend. Right there, though I didn't know how or to what purpose, in fact, wasn't even aware of it at the time (nor would I begin to appreciate the implications for another twenty years), but right there, I joined (or *re*joined) a family of pilgrims in pursuit of a particular light — call it art, call it alchemy, call it science, or call it God — a light that is nowhere at the same time it is everywhere. I had the sensation of being chosen, for what and by whom I had no clues.

I was shaking. I felt foolish, afraid I might cry. Some hysterical heart-wrenching tide of pain and joy was breaking loose in me and I was helpless to stop it (wouldn't if I could). She understood about these things. She pulled me closer and let me do what I needed to do.

The next time I woke up it was early morning, the park was empty, the Hall shut down, and I was alone, clutching the shawl in my hand. (I still have that shawl locked away in a trunk somewhere.)

*

I'd Been Warned
{^}

I'd been warned, told, and shown: to be careful, not to go on if the roads were bad, and how to negotiate a slide should I hit black ice; that last, from my step dad, more to terrorize my mother than to assist me in any real way. I had a new car, new to me at least — a '56 Chevy, stick shift, V-8, turquoise and white. I just wanted to get in it and drive. Going to see my dad was a legitimate excuse.

It was cold and windy, after dark before I finally got away from Tulsa. It was already beginning to drizzle. But I had good tires, a good heater, and carried a sleeping bag in the trunk. I'd be fine. Mother knew son would be fine. My step dad was just glad to be rid of me for a few days, and I was certainly glad to be going.

I hadn't gone ten miles before the drizzle turned to sleet, and soon after that to snow. By the time I crossed the state line into Arkansas, it was packed three inches deep on the road and still coming down. I hadn't seen another car for an hour. The last thirty miles into Bentonville were treacherous. I *loved* it. I've always enjoyed extreme weather, of almost any kind — something to scrape residue off the soul and enliven the senses, my dad used to say. It was mid-December, between semesters, and I hadn't seen my dad in two years, maybe three. He had a new house and a new family.

Coming into town I passed a hitchhiker going the other way. In the wind and swirling snow he looked almost ghostlike, and oddly familiar. At the time, I thought nothing of it.

It was late in the evening. My dad was waiting up, but his wife and kids — he had two small ones and another on the way — were already asleep. We hugged and laughed, remembered our life together and told stories while I ate a bowl of beans and cornbread.

I recalled the time when I was eight years old and he stood me on a milk crate facing the window, told me to watch for cars while he and two men loaded whiskey out the backdoor and into the trunk of a waiting car. The driveway was long and twisty and lined with trees. I was supposed to yell out if I saw headlights coming. I'm sure he never meant for me to be there, but what the hey, it was 'business' and I just happened to be visiting. This is the same story I retell each time we see each other after a lengthy absence. He always laughs and shakes his head at his own foolishness, embarrassed, I guess. But it has never been an embarrassment to me, never anything more than a window into a self-made man, good or bad, a blue-collar boy who could afford a tailor. My dad thought of himself as working class, but no one could remember ever seeing him do any. He was a gambler, an entrepreneur, an inventor of sorts, continuously reinventing himself to fit some imagined role. But he could never remember the role for very long. A little more consciousness, or a little less, might have saved him. As it was, he suffered.

I finished off a slice of red onion and went up to my room. It was a little after midnight. I could see by the streetlight that it was still snowing. It was like snow falling in a dream, literally. I remember hearing somewhere that snow falling in a dream indicates the presence of spirit. It was that kind of snow, with flakes the size of tiny doilies. And tree branches glistening like glass. I pulled the covers up to my ears and went to sleep immediately, which is rare for me. I don't know how long I slept, but I was awakened by a noise of some kind, something in the room. It took a moment for me to realize that I had fallen into one of those holes in sleep from which you wake yourself whimpering.

I jerked upright in bed. A faint humming noise tickled the air, like a breeze blowing through a field of wasps. More than that was a vibratory feeling moving through my body like a pneumatic drill. The room was filled with a dozen or so live *beings* looking like cylinders of light, and tall, very tall, seven feet or more. Terrified, I tried to yell out but couldn't make a sound.

If this next seems implausible that's only because it is true. And while I don't claim to understand any of the goings on, I do swear by it.

This tall being of light took me right through the wall and I was too stunned and afraid to resist or utter a word. On the other side of the wall *this* world melted away and was replaced by an environment so absolutely foreign to me that to this day I am unable to finds words to describe it; and without words or images it began immediately to fall out of memory. But I remember being told that I was going to see my real father — even though I was perfectly happy with the one I had, flaws and all.

I seemed to be lifted up into the arms of something or someone, and told that I was his son. I was told that my earth parents had been selected for me but that I was, in fact, one of them, one of the light beings. I was told that I was not altogether unique in this, just one of many. These beings were 'guardians' and were always in contact with me, though not always directly or in ways I might recognize and understand. All of these beings had children on earth, children who would grow up in apparently normal ways but with tasks to perform, and, at a future date, when some major planetary event was to occur, all of the children would suddenly know who they were and be able to communicate with one another. (My only thought at the time was that this is just too fucking real.)

Then it was over, just like that. I was unnerved but unharmed. I felt like I'd been cast out of an absolutely perfect but unknown place. The room was cold and dark. Outside, I could see that it had stopped snowing. I remember wondering if I'd been dreaming. If it was a dream, it certainly didn't feel like one; it felt like something that had been going on all along without me, and I'd only just rejoined whatever it was. It had the familiarity of place, as though it belonged to a geographical location to which I traveled in my helpless hours of unconsciousness. I remember thinking too, that there is a world of difference between having a dream (that may or may not be a dream) in which you see what you think to be aliens, and being told that you yourself might in some way be alien to the human race.

I wrestled around for another hour, couldn't get back to sleep, dressed finally, and went downstairs as soon as it was light. My dad came down a few minutes later and put on a pot of coffee. He asked if I had slept well, but the look in his eye suggested that he knew better. He didn't say anything, however. And neither did I. He stepped onto the back porch and stood looking at the snow and ice on the trees. It promised to be a cold, clear day.

Now, my dad always looked a little guilty of something — not darkly so, but sheepishly, as though he just might break into mischief at any moment and there was not a thing he or anyone could do about it. This morning he was quieter than usual, almost thoughtful. He poured us each a cup of coffee then left me drinking mine while he went out to buy cigarettes and some groceries for breakfast. He borrowed my new car to do it.

And never came back.

Several hours later his girlfriend called to say that he was crazy, he was in jail over in Noel, and could someone come and get him. My uncle drove over to the police station in Noel, and confirmed that my dad was indeed there, but he doubted if he was any crazier than he'd ever been. Apparently he'd gotten into a fight with his girlfriend's boyfriend, and had broken the nose of a policeman who was trying to break it up. And so on.

I was distraught, heartbroken, near to tears, wondering if or when I would ever see my new car again. And then there was my dad. In that moment I was inclined to agree with my uncle and stepmother: let the sunuvabitch rot in jail, she insisted, if I can't have him put to sleep can I at least have him neutered, just what the hell can I do?

In the end, she railed so much she turned my uncle to my dad's favor. But it was too late. There would be no bail. And no arraignment before Monday. Besides, my dad wasn't ready to come home yet. He'd made some new friends, and they were heavy into a domino game that promised to last out the weekend. Nor could he remember ever having been in jail before. He was curious to see what was so attractive about it. He'd be home the first of the week, he said. Or something like that. I'm sorry, but I have to confess that one of us was simple, and the other, *way* too complicated.

In all honesty I don't believe my dad was a dissatisfied man, nor even a promiscuous one. He simply could not learn the lines he'd scripted for himself. It was almost like he was trying to learn a foreign language by reading bits and scraps of newspapers he found in the street.

There was nothing left for me to do but hang around and build short snowmen for two children who seemed more puzzled than pleased. I shoveled the walk, helped put up a Christmas tree, ate beans, and watched daytime television: endless game shows and programs on the Nativity. That night, my stepmother put the kids to bed early, then lit candles and sat on the kitchen floor and drew a chalk circle around herself to protect herself from elementals, she said. And besides, it's better than sticking your head in an oven.

That second night was shadowy and full of games. At one point I woke up and thought there was a fireplace in my room. I saw myself by the fire, first as a child, then as a man, finally as something I couldn't identify. I got up to put out the fire, realized there wasn't one, and crawled back under the covers. I refused to go back to sleep after that, for fear I might wake up dreaming again.

My uncle surprised me the next morning by showing up with my car. The roads were open all the way into Oklahoma, he said, but another storm was on the way. I crawled all over, under, and around my car. Everything seemed okay. I loaded up, ate another bowl of beans, hugged everyone all around, and was on my way back to Tulsa by mid-afternoon. I wondered if, when, or where I might see my father again.

Leaving town I passed what looked to be the same hitchhiker I'd passed two days before. He was standing in the same spot, heading in the same direction. I slowed to pick him up but when I looked into my rearview mirror there was no one there. I felt like I'd eaten way too many beans in the last forty-eight hours. I turned onto the highway and clouds were already blocking the sun. Then it started to snow.

*

Higher Learning
{^}

Did you ever see yourself in a dream? I mean, walk up behind someone thinking it was someone else and when they turned around it was you? Unnerving. I've had whole days like that.

On this particular day, I felt like I was sitting just out of sight of something I couldn't imagine and wasn't at all sure I *wanted* to imagine.

This was in Fayetteville, early in the spring semester at the University of Arkansas, still winter in the Ozarks. I was sitting in a café on Division Street watching snow pile up outside the window when Prune came up to me disguised as a waiter. He set the table, lit a candle, filled my water glass, and opened his fist right in front of my face. In the palm of his hand was this little glass ball which, he pointed out, is something a person has or doesn't have, but only the one who has it has it, by god. Then he walked away without taking my order and came back a minute later with exactly what I wanted.

Holy shit, I'm thinking, *here we go again!*

Things were about to change and I knew it, I just didn't know how fast or in what way. So I was sitting there eating buttered toast and drinking hot chocolate, waiting for the snow to let up and the field house to open. I was just days away from becoming a fugitive. But I didn't know that yet.

I had not done particularly well at the U of A. Oh, I tested well, made decent grades, had even finagled myself an athletic scholarship. I was, I guess, a little smarter than I looked, but not as smart as I thought I was. I went to class, took copious notes, memorized details, but the truth is, I had no idea what was going on most of the time. Entire class periods passed without my understanding anything that was said. One of my professors even questioned whether or not I had been educated on this planet. And when I couldn't remember the words to the Declaration of Independence but claimed to know what our founding fathers 'intended' as they argued over its wording, more than that, I even knew what was on each one's mind as he said it — well, that was information my history professor had no use for. And if I couldn't prove it, or show him where I'd read it, then would I please shut up about it. That's what he said.

It depressed me to be so...irrelevant. When I wasn't in class or at the field house, I hid out in the music building, tinkering on the piano. I had a girlfriend back in Tulsa, a fiancé, sort of, but there was too much distance between us; we'd both lost interest. Still, having her 'in the bank' saved me the embarrassment of having to talk or make conversation with hot, spanky, college girls. Not that I didn't want one of those hot, spanky college girls, I just didn't know how to go about it. So most of my spare time was spent in the field house playing basketball with other members of the football team, all of us waiting for spring practice to start.

These intra-squad basketball games between football players were a tradition, a way of staying in shape in the off-season without actually putting on the pads. The idea was to square off against your competition whenever you could, just to see what the two of you were made of. It could be brutal at times. In fact, it had become box office stuff, other students on campus willing to pay two or three bucks just to watch the spectacle --- part basketball, part mayhem, and all joke. We looked like two teams of rodeo clowns.

My competition was a kid named Chuck Tempher. Chuck was three or four inches taller than me, and fifty pounds heavier. But I was fast, so fast I ran circles around him on the court. And I could jump clear over his head if need be. That was my claim to fame: I could run and I could jump. Both of those things he found irritating.

For whatever reason, no one seemed to like Chuck. He had no sympathizers, no cohorts, no one in his corner. Even his own teammates encouraged me, and got a kick out of it when I showed him up. Some were openly hostile to Chuck, but most of them just wanted to be in on his humiliation without getting in harm's way.

He was big but he was soft, a pussy, a momma's boy, you could tell that by listening to him whine. And he made good grades easily. That pissed me off.

On this particular day I stole the ball from Chuck a few times, hit a couple of jumpers. Then I drove around him and put the ball over the rim with both hands. Slick, I thought. Nifty. Chuck just glared at me and shook his head. Then a pout came over his face and that's when I knew I had him. I felt invincible. I had fast hands, fast feet, the crowd on my side. I was going to give him a beating, the beating of his life, and right in front of all our teammates, the coaches, everyone.

I don't know exactly how it started, but I guess I threw the first punch. Chuck threw the next one, the last, as it turned out. I went down like a bag of cement.

*

Now, what is real and what is unreal is determined by consensus. The conviction that our version of reality is correct and someone else's is an illusion usually stems from the fact that there are more of us than there are of them. On the other hand, just because you don't know what a thing is doesn't mean it's not what it is.

I don't remember much of the last few minutes before the fight, or anything for the next three days after. I was unconscious, in a coma, I guess; the damage caused less by Chuck's punch to my chin, as to the way in which my head bounced off the hardwood floor. For months the back of my head felt like a bruised cantaloupe.

I woke up in the hospital with no recollection of how I'd gotten there or that I had, in fact, been there for three days and nights. During that time I had a long and lucid dream in which I moved seamlessly from one real state into another, equally real, and was taken on a journey by something or someone I couldn't identify — an intelligence of sorts, but nothing I could later make sense of. On this journey I was shown planets that seemed to be of our solar system, including a tenth one out beyond Neptune and Pluto, which had not yet been discovered. Then I was taken to another star system deep in space and introduced to several beings, each with a different perspective on the universe, different truths, different laws, and different ways of processing information.

Each being seemed to be unique to its environment, but I can't for the life of me tell you what any one of them looked like. I wondered if perhaps we were on some sort of spacecraft but was told, no, nothing quite like that; we were, instead, inside something they called a 'phase-resonator' — a vibratory space between dimensions. And they communicated telepathically, without words or movement. Wherever I was, it seemed more real than anything I had ever experienced in my life, waking or sleeping.

I was told that my hosts were actually explorers attempting to contact other life-forms for the purpose of recruiting ambassadors, messengers sent to inspire the local inhabitants to a higher form of consciousness. More specifically, we were being made to remember our lineage — *who* we are, *what* we are, *where* we came from, and *why* — a lineage that appears to come from star systems deep in the universe, but is only just beginning to resonate in our DNA as memories. Dormant aspects of our neural circuitry were being 'triggered' at this time, bringing about a gradual change of consciousness.

The only hitch in the process is that it must be done while the mind is in a certain state of consciousness, and that means switching awareness off during the communication. This, they said, is because of the difference in time *here* and time *there*. The result is that the subject appears to be in a deep and irreversible coma, perhaps for minutes, perhaps for years — in my case, for three days and nights. And once you are returned to local waking consciousness you have no memory of having been spacenapped at all.

This otherworld (alien?) intelligence has apparently been here and influencing the human species for a long time, maybe as long as there's been human intelligence. I don't know. (And they were quick to point out that 'alien' doesn't necessarily mean another star system; it might not even mean another planet. It might simply mean another dimension or vibratory phase — anything 'alien' to the status quo of consciousness and ego.)

Thirty years later and a universe away, I am only just beginning to make the necessary hookups in consciousness to remember any of what took place during those three days and nights in the hospital. I guess you could say I am just coming out of the coma. At the time, I had few clues and no answers.

I woke up in a dark room with two shadows standing over me, *corporeal* shadows.

One shadow belonged to Chuck Tempher, the other, to a nurse we'll call Wanda (not her real name).

*

I stayed in the hospital another four days and nights — was there when my fiancé showed up to see if I was alive and well, and to return my engagement ring. I guess that should have added to my misery, and I did my best to appear crushed and crestfallen, but in fact, I was relieved.

My life before all this had definite boundaries, limited memories to draw from. I thought I knew who and what I wanted to be, what it would take to get there, even knew the person I would sail off into the future with. But in a single moment all that had changed. My athletic career was over; my formal education would be interrupted for a decade, whatever plans I had for the future had been drastically rerouted. I felt like I had fallen asleep with one memory bank, and woke up with another — my own and someone else's. I would never again, at least not in any immediate future, know who I was for certain. I didn't know it at the time, but I was about to spend the next twenty years on a search for something or someone I couldn't be sure existed.

And that's where Wanda comes in. A dark-eyed, bosomy thing with really long legs, Wanda was on duty the night I was admitted to the hospital. She was on night duty that entire week, her last week, as fate would have it. She'd actually given her notice a month earlier.

In the middle of the night, after her chores were done and things had settled down on her floor, she came into my room. Sometimes she read to me. Sometimes she talked. And sometimes she just watched me sleep. She had deep-set, watchful eyes. Even when she smiled I felt her taking my measure, felt the force of her curiosity. It wasn't an arrogant curiosity: she wanted to know who I was. To be looked at that way is unsettling when you feel vulnerable and in danger of being seen through and exposed. I wasn't sure what private part of me was open to exposure, but I knew I didn't want just anyone looking at it.

To mitigate my fears, Wanda told me her story:

It seems that when she was young and growing up in Missouri, she'd been one of a pack of hysterically miserable girls who ran around in tight clothes, plastered their faces with makeup, chain-smoked, talked in class, and did their best to catch the attention of boys who would be sure to use them badly. One of them knocked her up. After a difficult pregnancy, the baby, a boy, was stillborn, and during the birth Wanda herself had actually died. She was only dead for a minute or two then came back. It was long enough for her to pass though the 'tunnel,' into the light, the whole bit.

When Wanda came back from being dead, she was a different person.

She was a 'walk-in.' One usually becomes a walk-in after some emotional trauma or near-death experience, explained Wanda. It's sort of like being possessed by a friendly spirit — nothing dark or disturbing like that of the *Exorcist* or *The Three Faces of Eve*, but a high-minded entity who is permitted to take over the body of another human being who wishes to depart, a *benevolent* spirit, with humanitarian motivations, helping others to help themselves; a spirit with a mission. Wanda's job was very specific but I never fully understood it. As near as I could make out, she was some sort of angel, an expression of the Divine Mother come all this way to tell me something I'd come all this way to hear, or so she said. I'm thinking: *God damn, God's ways are wild when compared to ours!*

I had all sorts of questions. And Wanda's answers were carefully thought out. She seemed to be checking some invisible notebook before each answer, making sure it was right, and only then giving it up: a process done at lightning speed, but a process nonetheless.

A walk-in, huh. I had to think about it. Most religions seem to accept the concept of possession by devils. Why not then be possessed by saints and angels?

Wanda explained that no entity can take over another without permission, there are no accidents or forced takeovers. As a walk-in, you inherit the karma of the body you inhabit; and that can sometimes be confusing, not to mention frustrating — it's not always easy to tell what is yours and what belongs to the other. Not that it matters; you have to first complete the tasks of the previous owner before you go on to your own projects. Of course, you get full use of the memory and training left behind. But you'll probably not consciously know you are a walk-in until the time is right. That might take years. In the meantime, she said, it is more important to learn than to always do the right thing.

There are at least two kinds of walk-ins, said Wanda, maybe more. But two she knew of: those from the human family, come here from the sixth dimension to assist in uplifting the consciousness of the species and perhaps help them survive the human condition — she hinted at both natural and manmade disasters to come. And then there are the so-called extraterrestrials, the family of light she called them, the star people. They seem to have come here from another space or place, perhaps another galaxy. Their immediate purpose is one of exploration and research throughout the local universe, she said. But even as she said it, I was having my own thoughts:

Indeed, I could hear a voice, Prune's or my own, talking about things to which I had no clues: it seemed to suggest something of a *pre*-human existence, perhaps as light beings ourselves, come here to create a new species, a new planetary being. In doing so, we (or they) volunteered to inhabit the entire human species in order to walk them (or us) through the birth process, midwife to the new human. As we search for answers and enlightenment, with each discovery the human species wakes up a little more, *aha!* It's the 'hundredth-monkey' thing: the more of us who know, and are willing to share what we know, the more the species is changed.

And so on. Information continued to pour out of me that I didn't know I had; couldn't *imagine*, but couldn't turn off either, some deep wake-up call, causing me to remember things I didn't know I knew. I felt like the whole world was a television left on in the corner of the room, and the room was my head. Of course I can't prove any of this. But then, even Einstein, if he came back today, couldn't *prove* that space and time are curved. My only concern, then or now, is to tell the truth without labeling myself a lunatic. And it doesn't take a forklift operator to figure out that a voice in your head saying, *I am your alter ego from another universe,* is not necessarily to be trusted, and you might be wise to avoid operating heavy machinery until it goes away.

Understand now, all of this was going on in my head, I wasn't actually saying a word. Suddenly I became aware of a profound silence in the room.

Only then did I realize that Wanda wasn't talking either, hadn't been for several minutes. She was smiling. Watching me. I had the distinct impression that she had stopped talking in order to pay closer attention to what was going on in my head. It was quiet for a long time. Then she left.

*

More and more my life was angling off toward the weird unknown. Even I could see that. Still, I felt protected. I knew I was being saved for...something. My frustration was in not knowing what, not an inkling, not a clue. And no matter what I fell into, I seemed to always come away with a gift of some sort, some personal treasure I might not have come across otherwise. Wanda was just such a gift.

The following night was her last on the job before she struck off for parts unknown. She was a nurse-gypsy and a bonafide angel. Her eyes were the color of a raven's wing, but one eye had a slight cast and didn't track well. Instead of awkward, it made her look charming and vulnerable. She was, perhaps, a bit frayed around the edges, but she was beautiful. The kind of woman you think about while you're doing it with someone else.

When she came into my room that last night, I was ready for her. I'd been ready for days. I was lonely and depressed and feeling somewhat sentimental. I admit to having felt lonely and depressed for quite some time, but this sudden urge to sentiment was brought on by Wanda.

She was an amazing creature, what with that face and those eyes and all that bosomy stuff; not to mention those long legs. And holy? Lord knows not all angels are created equal.

I lay there, naked and pretending to sleep, feeling my heart swell and my sentiment take on new and unexpected proportions.

She didn't say a word at first. She emptied the trash, swept the floor, replaced the water in my glass and the soup in my bowl, then prepared to change the bed with me still in it, all the time thinking her own thoughts, which were several. For one, she thought she was only twenty years old. Which she wasn't. For another, she thought I was an Indian. Which I'm not. Also, she must've been thinking a little about the same things I was thinking about.

But none of this was apparent on her face. Instead, she seemed to be very intimate with something going on that nobody else could see. And she did not look the least bit sentimental.

Nevertheless, when Wanda backed out of the bathroom, mopping the floor as she went, I made my move. It was not a particularly romantic move, but effective, nonetheless.

She turned around and told me not to hurt myself, indicating the bandage on my head and the i.v. dangling from my arm. I hoisted her up as best I could and she wrapped her legs around my waist. Somehow, I managed to flip off the lights, lock the door, and wrench my back, before I twisted my ankle on a discarded shoe and fell on the bed, into Wanda, knocking the wind out of both of us. "It's never like this in the movies," I said.

"No," she whispered, laughing softly, "there just isn't room enough in those narrow seats." And I fell deeply, madly, temporarily in love with her forever.

We rolled around a bit, repositioning ourselves for greater intimacy. Then this most amazing thing happened, and for a second I thought I was seeing double. "Can you love me in two places at once?" she said. I thought she was suggesting some sort of sexual gymnastic. But that's not what she meant at all. "Love all of me," she said. And for a moment there were several of us; I mean, several of her and several of me. It was like watching an image caught in facing mirrors. Each image was doing the same thing to the other, but in slightly different ways. And there seemed to be multiple sources of feeling, as if I could touch what each image was doing in the mirror. "*Not yet! Not yet!*" she cried, and I could feel myself inside her, the moistness and all; at the same time she was doing a dozen different things with my cock. It made no sense, but it didn't matter. I stopped caring if my senses were true to anything I understood or had previously experienced. I just knew I was about to have an orgasm in several places at once.

*

Later that night, as Wanda prepared to leave for good, I begged her to take me with her. But she'd have no part of it. Said I needed to recuperate before I went anywhere. And that I couldn't very well go where she was going since she didn't know herself where that was — Seattle, perhaps, maybe San Francisco. We exchanged numbers and addresses where we might be traced. (I actually caught up with her years later on the Olympic Peninsula in Washington, but by then we were both other people.)

She left and I fell strangely, sweetly asleep, only to wake up a minute later with Prune standing over me in his pure essence. He placed a marble-sized crystal in the palm of my hand and made me promise to keep a secret, then left without telling me what that secret was.

I lay there for another hour, wondering if perhaps I was losing my mind. Wondering, so what? Then I got up and put on my clothes and removed the bandage from my head. Just before dawn, I slipped out of the hospital. It was cold and blustery, clouds stretched like brains across the sky. Without a word to anyone, I left school, left home, left the world as I had come to know it. The only proof I had of the whole experience was a soft spot the size of a grapefruit on the back of my head, and a tiny crystal I carried in my pocket. I figured, what the hell, only the one who has it has it, and I've certainly got whatever it is.

*

Breakout
{^}

After slipping away from the hospital in Fayetteville, I went home thinking to take a vacation from myself.

But home no longer felt like home. It was like I'd gone to sleep in one place and woke up in another. Nothing was familiar. I was restless and irritable. I knew that somewhere there was an explanation for what was going on with me. I had a lifetime of clues and innuendos but nothing coherent I could latch on to. And since I didn't know what exactly I was looking for, or where to go to find it, I just packed a bag, put my thumb in the air, and went. I had thirty-five dollars in my pocket when I left home, and no destination.

My first ride took me all the way to Kansas, so I guess I was headed north, more or less. Coming out of Wichita I got a ride with a kindly middle-aged accountant who just wanted to show me some pictures and touch my leg. In those days I thought a homosexual was some sort of furry creature indigenous to the Canadian Rockies. (I didn't really believe that, but that's what I'd been educated to believe.) I pretended not to understand, resisted his timid advances for a couple of hours, and got out at an intersection just east of Topeka.

Beneath a dark sky and scattered sheets of lightening, I headed east, to Kansas City, where I spent two days with a high school buddy of mine, and a third with his wife.

From Kansas City I went north to Omaha, and turned left.

Outside of North Platt, Nebraska I stopped for three days to shovel manure and pitch hay with a half-dozen real cowboys in real cowboy hats on a real ranch. It was hot, dry, dusty, all the usual. I figured I could do just about anything as long as I knew I didn't have to do it forever. But on the morning of the fourth day, my back ached, my legs ached, and I could not get the shit out from under my fingernails. So I quit. Just refused to get up. I slept until noon then lounged around the rest of the day and stole away that evening after dark, after dinner, and after much verbal abuse from those real cowboys in their real hats with real shit on their leathery souls. I was too humiliated to even pick up my pay.

Understand, Prune was with me all this time. Not always in my line of sight but never far away, he changed disguises constantly, and wouldn't abandon me for a minute. He tasted my food and water, kept a measured distance but watched over me while I slept, giving rise to the rumor that he was my secret lover while in fact he was much more than that. (I didn't try to explain him to anyone; didn't even bother acknowledging his existence.)

In Wyoming I stopped in Laramie and spent all but my last two dollars on a cowboy hat of my own. I visited a pool hall in Medicine Bow, two bars in Casper, and a café in Shoshoni, on my way to the Yellowstone, I thought, kind of. Ended up sleeping in a deep ditch somewhere outside of Jackson Hole surrounded by Tetons and bears — a magic land carved out of time and something graceful.

Sometime in the night the winds came up and a cold rain fell, half snow. I woke up wet but exhilarated, oddly joyful. *Why is there something, rather than nothing,* I wrote in a small notebook for reasons I understood then and am less sure about now. It was still dark and I walked for two hours before I finally caught a ride with a farmer in a blue pickup who offered to take me wherever I needed to go; that, without even knowing where I was going. I was suspicious, especially since I wasn't sure myself.

He turned out to be a sheep farmer from Alpine, on his way to market. He seemed harmless enough, and I slid into the seat beside him while Prune climbed into the truck bed along with the sheep and goats and whatever-in-hell else was back there.

A crusty old fart with bushy white hair and gray eyes, the farmer tried to tell me he was some sort of holy man, a converted something or other, not sure what. Over the course of the next few hours I found out that he dearly loved drinking wine, eating red meat, and making love to women, beautiful or otherwise; his vocabulary was absolutely vile; not a passive holy person by any stretch, certainly nothing my aunt would approve of. He had a sort of ornery independence about him — an animal with dignity, like a lion or an elephant. It occurred to me that only a soul possessed of great Spirit and a heavenly vision could comprehend and do justice to such debauchery.

He was, I guess, an unholy-holy man. All his drinking buddies were spiritual aspirants, he said. Even when we're drunk we talk about the VOID.

He advised me not to try so hard to make sense of things. If you can make sense of your life, he said, then you're using your mind. Life is not some wonderful machine that kicks in at birth, then relentlessly moves on for six or seven decades, following laws that you've made up. Life does make sense, but it doesn't give a damn about your laws. As for 'reality,' he said, you create reality by simply *living* your life. It's not a separate job you apply for.

Then he confessed to being an extraterrestrial.

Actually, he said he was an 'other-dimensional,' but led me to believe they were one and the same. Either way, it irritated me enough to get my attention.

He claimed to be an other-dimensional under contract to perform certain tasks while occupying this body, which, incidentally, didn't belong to him. It was a loaner. That's what he said. He'd agreed to come into a body that was something of a wreck and a nuisance, and to do things he didn't always enjoy, just for the experience of being alive in the third-dimension. All life is intelligent, he said, even human life.

He answered a lot of questions I didn't ask, and told me things he thought I needed to know, things I didn't know enough about to even be curious. He led me to believe that aliens are real, but not their spaceships, not exactly. They're not necessary, exactly. Most of our 'visitors' are simply molecular alterations from a dimension next door — beings that co-exist with us right here on earth. No need to look to the heavens, he said, just look inside. He told me that the real point of being abducted is not to serve as some intergalactic guinea pig, nor is it to act as something special in the cosmic plan — no messiahs, no archetypal gods or goddesses. No matter how it might manifest, there is just one thing going on everywhere, and that's the raising of consciousness on the planet, yours, mine, everyone's.

And so on. He continued to fill my head with stuff and minutiae I had no use for at the time, didn't understand, didn't want to hear. A lot of what he said echoed my own past experiences, but some of it was so foreign that I wondered if he might not be speaking another language. Most disturbing was the fact that everything he said, while not making any rational sense, resonated in my heart.

But I just wanted to know who or what's been messing with me as far back as I can remember.

He looked at me square and winked. It's a conspiracy, he said. There are beings out there conspiring to bring you blessings and make you smart.

When he pulled onto the shoulder to drop me off, I got out quietly and slipped away, leaving Prune asleep in the back of the truck.

*

Later that same day I learned to make soup out of catsup, crackers, sugar, and a glass of water. This was in Ogden, Utah. And I never did get to Yellowstone, not for another three years, anyway.

Instead, I opted for a seven-day joy ride to Las Vegas with two sisters who were just off on a lark, away from friends, family, husbands, all that. A glorious week in which I leaned how to, first, 'do it like a goat,' and later, to 'do it like earthworms.' I never learned their real names or where they were from, only that their destination was Albuquerque, and that didn't interest me.

For the next few weeks I hitched around, bummed around, cooled my feet in Lake Mead, swam in the Colorado

River, hiked in and out of the Grand Canyon, fell asleep in the backseat of a red convertible, and woke up on the desert floor outside of Needles in an electrical storm, a noisy, clattering, scary kind of night which left even the animals in the desert scurrying around looking for a place to hide.

All that manic mobility came to a screeching halt when I got arrested in Tucson, Arizona for 'suspicion.'

Suspicion of *what* was never made clear. But a dead man was involved. And my fingerprints were all over him. In fact, I was going through his pockets when the police drove up. It was like this:

I was hitchhiking across the Sonora Desert and arrived in Tucson late at night, too late to go on, I thought. It was windy, with dust and sand and trash blowing everywhere, lightening in the distance. And I was walking the streets looking for a sheltered place to roll out my sleeping bag and sleep for the night, when I saw a man back out of a doorway and stumble up the street in my direction, then fall, almost at my feet. I bent down and turned him over, but there was no helping him up. A black man about my age, he lay in a pool of blood, a steak knife buried in his sternum. I held his head in my lap and looked around, frantically, for someone, anyone, help of any kind. The streets were strangely empty, and quiet — nothing but the wind and the dust. I leaned closer and tried to comfort him. There was no pain on his face, no fear. He smiled and seemed to recognize me, that, or something over my shoulder and behind me that I couldn't see. His tongue lolled from his mouth as he tried to speak, and he gave me a look filled with an emotion I have never experienced in myself or seen in another. Then with a *woosh!* it all went out of him and he went limp in my arms. I looked up and a shape was close to my face. It was like a shadow swimming in air, or a shimmer of heat from a hot road in summer, only fainter, and quite cool. It felt like a breeze had brushed my cheek. I remember thinking, *my god, it's his soul.* All that in a flash of a second, then it disappeared.

I was unable to move, in shock, I guess, everything happened so fast. I may have been crying a little; not for him especially, certainly not for myself, but for something I couldn't identify. My heart felt open in a way that I'd never experienced it, open and full and torn, all at the same time.

I was going through his pockets, looking for some identification, when the police drove up and arrested me. Jailed again. And that, because there was no one else around, just me, holding a dead man in my arms.

*

At the station house I was booked, labeled a transient, then grilled by two cops who took turns playing good-cop, bad-cop with my head. One of them was tall, thin, handsome, neat, and pasty looking. He actually looked sticky. The other cop was a goon. He had a crew cut, no neck, and a six-inch gap between his eyes. A pair of repressed homosexuals who were, I imagine, more comfortable in a barracks than a boudoir. I read later where one of them actually went into politics. And did well.

He told me that I made him sick; that I was a beatnik and I made him want to throw up. He said he would see to it personally that I got thirty years, maybe even life. I wondered what my mother would say. I wondered, how many times can you call home and say you're in jail? Thirty years. It sounded like such a long time. It seemed like I'd been alive forever, yet I was just twenty years old. I added ten years to that and tried to imagine it.

For several hours, I was alternately bullied and then left alone to stew in solitude; all this, while they called around about my identity. I had an old picture on an old health card leftover from a job I had once. But they said it didn't look like me, and I had to agree. It was a dumb picture. My head was on from left to right instead of right to left. I looked younger and more innocent than anyone has a right to look.

I hadn't had a shave or a haircut in weeks, so they gave me one; removed every hair from my adam's apple to the nape of my neck. If I looked disgusting and unkempt before, now I looked scary. After filling my head with fuck stories and local folklore, they put me into a cell by myself, to think about things. I had a flush-hole in there, and a metal cot, a thin mattress, a roll of toilet paper, and a bar of soap made out of gravel. It could be worse, I thought. That, before it got worse.

It was quiet on the cellblock. A few cells were occupied but no one said anything, not even the jailer. He just grunted and let me into my cell. He was not a sadist. For the most part he ignored me, and I appreciated that. My thoughts were flying around like leaves in a firestorm. I needed to be alone with them — better yet, *without* them, without any thought at all. I felt a little queasy in the stomach, kind of feverish. I stretched out on the hard mattress, clasped my hands behind my head, and stared at the ceiling, flat and white, with a 25-watt bulb hanging from it unprotected. And that was curious. Light bulbs in these places are usually encased in little wire cages. And never left to dangle. Before I had time to wonder about it, the air was suddenly sucked from my lungs, my body became rooted in the mattress, and the light bulb seemed to fall right out of the ceiling into my face. Just above my forehead it stopped falling, dangled there for a moment, then began to sparkle, then it turned blue, then it turned into a soft white moon that entered my head and *exploded* in a million tiny electrical shocks running up and down my arms and legs and spine, into my knees, my navel, in my throat, on my tongue. I saw snakes. I heard songs, bells in the background, and religious music. I wanted to scream or break into a rage as that soft white moon turned into a fire and whipped against my asshole (coccyx, actually.) I couldn't breathe. But strangely enough, even with all that was going on, I felt no real alarm. And that was alarming.

I closed my eyes. Then I opened them. Then I closed them again. I seemed to be fully conscious and cognizant, witnessing a state of madness in my own head. And I didn't even wonder about it. I had no clues where my thoughts were coming from or where my mind might go next. Jailed in Tucson, impaled to my cot, not breathing, alert but not alarmed, and all I could wonder about was my lack of wonder.

I couldn't even remember my name, or where I left off and everything else began. People I didn't know on streets I didn't recognize seemed to be moving gently and steadily around the edges of my periphery. They weaved and swarmed and wrapped themselves together into one long flowing rope then made their way into the roots and plants and trees disguised as the inward flow of sap. Everything was just...*energy*...one thing expressing itself in different ways.

I made my way along the veins and arteries of some internal root system, swimming with the flow of whatever it was, until I surfaced, finally, in a universe parallel to the one I was accustomed to — similar, but somehow different. I seemed to have borrowed someone else's memory-bank and landed in a different jail cell.

This 'other' cell was, in fact, a repository of information buried deep inside my own etheric brain system. However, because I was incapable of 'thinking' of it that way, it was made to resemble a jail cell next door to the one I was in.

It was after midnight when the gentle jailer moved me into a different cell. It was almost dark in there. And quiet — a religious quiet, full of presence and ominous portent. And I was not alone. Sitting on the lower bunk, a sock in one hand, doing something religious with the other, was a genuine jailbird. I'd never seen one up close before. He was disguised as a Comanche Indian. He wore his hair pulled back in a long braid, and had a blue water turkey tattooed on his chest. Under all that, he looked more than a little familiar. I just knew I was gonna be sick.

The door clanged shut behind me and I stood there empty, desperate, almost suicidal, alone in the semi-dark with a stranger I could barely see and couldn't begin to imagine. He didn't look up or say a word. He didn't move. But his eyes rolled halfway open and a light momentarily flooded the room. When he closed them, it went dark again.

Suddenly I needed to shit in the worst way.

I climbed onto the top bunk, put my boots under my head, buried my face in my arm, and began to pray.

*

That night I dreamed I was having my limbs removed and my blood siphoned off.

Actually, it was the other memory-bank that had the dream. In it, Prune came into my cell without benefit of disguise. He bowed slightly to the Comanche jailbird, who bowed to him in turn. They seemed to know each other. Then Prune explained something to me that I couldn't really get a handle on: he told me that once upon a time I had been a dervish living in the Ural Mountains — I don't know if he meant in another life or on a different plane of existence — but I was a whirling dervish in danger of losing my soul to the dance. To prevent this happening, he, Prune, had driven a stake into my knee; and that was the cause of the terrible pain I was feeling at the moment. Then he'd driven a nail into my forehead, the second because the first made me suffer but didn't let me die. It was an act of compassion, he explained. And so on. I actually felt better after his explanation, peaceful and pain free. Then he said he was going to let me die a little, but not to be afraid. It'll be all right, he said. It would help me get through the next thing. And even as he said it, I felt the fear melt away and be replaced by an immense relief that grew deeper as my consciousness trickled away.

The next thing was some sort of shamanic ritual in which all my joints were forcibly disjointed, my flesh scraped, my body fluids drained off and flushed away, and my eyes torn from their sockets, all this with no panic, no real concern on my part. I seemed to be watching from across the room, even helping with the operation. My bones and body parts were then gathered up and somehow fashioned together again; my DNA was amped up, my electrical system rewired — I had a new brain. The sensation was that of being disassembled and transported to another dimension where I was then reassembled and made whole again. I felt wonderful, like I'd been taken to some marvelous place and shown some hidden thing that was amazing, forever amazing.

Like a stone into gold, I changed — rather, the other memory-bank changed, not me personally.

One of us came to in a jail cell, chilled and running a fever of the sort you think you just might die from, might even welcome. The in-house nurse was mopping my forehead with a wet cloth and applying ice packs. Prune was gone but the jailbird was still there. I didn't know where I was exactly, what world, what dimension, whose memory-bank even, or which side of the veil. I hoped I wasn't dead — this was no place to spend eternity.

After the nurse left, the Comanche jailbird spoke to me for the first time. You do good work, he said, and smiled. Then he told me his name was Breaks Wind (actually I could never pronounce his name, but that's what it sounded like, and that's how I've come to remember him.)

Breaks Wind was a religious craftsman, a shaman of sorts. His purpose was simply to sacralize reality; in other words, make sacred whatever forms, turns, twists and revolutions the mind of man makes on its way to revealing itself to itself. To that end, he said, he was there to teach me...something, and a lot of it; he just wasn't sure what.

He leaned forward on his bunk, handed me a sock, and began telling me what he knew about things like reality and awareness and enlightenment and hysteria, things he thought I needed to know.

But I was a hard sell. What with everything else going on, I told him I didn't really care to hear it. He told me he didn't care that I didn't care: I was in line to be told, and it didn't make a turd whether I wanted to hear it or not. He led me to believe that I was on someone's *list*. God's perhaps, but maybe not. In any event, it was *my turn*.

I couldn't stop him or tune him out. I felt helpless, sort of drugged and sleepy, but not about to pass out. He told me that this reality business is a tricky business, and getting stuck in one is as bad as getting stuck in any other.

I handed the sock back to him and asked if he would explain that.

He took the sock and said, no.

But he continued talking about things related and unrelated. He said something about balance in there somewhere, and the curative aspects of schizophrenia. I said something then, and he said something else. I'm afraid I don't remember much of what either of us had to say. I do remember him telling me that, in the beginning was the *Word* and the Word was God: everything after that is just rhetoric. He said, nothing has never happened before, memory is a bedpan for the soul, pain is a clock, sanity is a swinging door marked *Exit* on both sides, and about all that can be said for normal is that it's very fucking normal. Ah! but isn't it great to be in love when you're average.

He told me that good health is inert; that dissipation lies directly in the path of enlightenment, and sodomy is not a literary act. He asked if I knew that after death the soul goes to a cannery in Little Rock, Arkansas? I said no, I didn't know that. And he told me not to repeat it because he wasn't sure the world was ready for that one yet.

I wanted to know what, if he knew so damned much, was he doing in here?

He ignored the implication and handed me the sock while telling me that if I got too caught up in the things of this earth, too close to the people that inhabit it, I could get real sick and not even remember who I am.

Then he told me I was destined to spend the next seven years circling the globe collecting things of my self and remembering. Of course, I wanted to know what *things*, what *self*, but all he said was that each thing I remembered would cause the world around me to change. He told me that my primary function on this planet at this time is simply to create a data base for the new human; and that it didn't matter whether I got anything right or did everything wrong, mistakes are necessary to building a complete data base, he said. It is more important to learn than to always do the right thing. Then he smiled and warned me to watch closely the breathing of anyone who offered to give me information because only the one who knows the truth has the courage to lie about it. But no one has any answers, he said. There is as much of God to be found in the snatch of a woman's conversation as there is in a prophet's prattling. That's gospel, but I can't give you the exact scripture. Then he took the sock and asked if there was anything else I'd like to know that he might've overlooked?

Of course I wanted to know about UFOs and aliens and stuff like that, things I'd been driven by all my life.

Breaks Wind laughed and cautioned me against buying in to the appearance of things; the 'costume,' he called it. The beings entering your plane of existence have atomic structures different from yours. They have to make adjustments, make themselves look like something you'll believe, otherwise you'd never be open to what they have to say. Truth is, we are all the same thing doing the same thing in different ways.

Then he put the ritual sock away and informed me that this dream was about to reach closure, my education was over for the time being, enlightenment is best attained through hardship and struggle, and the word 'hysteria' comes from a Greek word meaning uterus. Oh, and by the way, he said, *consciousness* is the answer to your next question.

Until that moment, I didn't even know I had one.

*

Breaks Wind disappeared sometime in the night; perhaps he was furloughed. I don't know. What I do know is that I didn't hear from him again for three years. He and Prune were both with me in Alaska, on the island of Kodiak, when I came close to dropping the body I was involved with at the time. But that's another story. Best saved for another time.

I lay back on the cot with my hands behind my head, thinking about Breaks Wind thinking about me. I was staring up at a flat white ceiling with a light bulb hanging from it like a 25-watt moon, just inches from my face. And suddenly the breath returned to my body.

*

I was startled. Stunned. Not exactly fearful, but definitely concerned. I had no idea where I'd been or for how long, only that I wasn't asleep, hadn't *been* asleep. My legs ached. My back ached. My body was stiff as wood. Alone in a jail cell in Tucson, Arizona, I felt like I'd been trying all night to climb out of myself.

And if that wasn't enough, as I began to come back into my primary consciousness, I became aware of three light beings standing guard outside my cell — not to keep me in, but to keep whatever else out; I did not feel confined but protected. What happened next, is even more of a puzzle. And there is nothing in my journal, nothing in any available memory-bank to tell me *how* it happened:

Strangely at first, then impossibly, the cell began to break up and dissolve, then the building itself— no cops, no jailer, no Breaks Wind. Suddenly I found myself outside, and lying on the ground. I could feel sprinkles of rain on my face, the desert floor like warm flannel beneath me. The air smelled wet and musty and sweet, like only the desert can after a rain. Ball-lightening was bouncing around in the distance while overhead there were stars and stars and stars, faces floating by like helium balloons, my grandmother, my Aunt Juliet, Grandma Belle, Donnie in a hospital gown trailing tubes. The night was full of dead people and I was waiting for dawn to arrive. I have no idea how much time had passed — hours, days, weeks — but it was early morning and I was lying on my back in the middle of the Sonora Desert. I could feel someone watching me, whispering my name and the names of the constellations into my ear: Cygnus the Swan, Pegasus the Horse, the seven sisters of Pleiades, Cassiopeia, Arcturus, Canis Major the Great Dog, that's Sirius, your home planet. You are on planet Earth. *Wake up!*

*

Later that day, I was back on the road when I got word of Prune's disappearance.

I'd been hitchhiking all day, feeling exhilarated and nervous, looking over my shoulder, ducking into alleyways and ditches whenever I saw a patrol car approach. In a diner outside Sacramento I stopped to grab a sandwich and check the newspaper for anything on my escape. Nothing. Not a word.

But in a two-column story on the second page, I saw something else. According to the article, Prune had either been eaten by a bear or abducted by aliens; there was conjecture on both sides. Of course, they didn't mention him by name but I recognized him by a description of his belongings. It seems his boots, clothes, sleeping bag and an odd assortment of possessions had been discovered by a Forest Ranger hiking in the area of Mount Shasta. They were found in a circular clearing in the woods, stacked in a neat little pile with his underwear on top. There was a penciled note in one pants pocket that said: *It is better to be born ignorant than to achieve ignorance the hard way.* And went on to conclude that the secret to knowing is to not do what you know how to do to the things you know. He said: Drop your words. Drop your mind. Drop your dreams, your desperations, whatever you may be doing. Drop physics, metaphysics, your drawers, any idea you may have acquired about reality, drop it. The secret is that there is no secret. The universe is a hype. Reality is a crutch. We are all the same thing doing the same thing in different ways. I am holy. You are holy. It is all sacred. There are doors but no walls, keys but no locks. Come on in! It's just you and the tunnel forever. If there is a light somewhere, you're it.

*

But I was too young and that was too easy. I was convinced that something was going on in my life behind my back. At the same time, I believed that we create our own realities. I couldn't resolve the two feelings. So, for the next two decades I continued to search for something I didn't know the name of and didn't always recognize when I found it. Too long in any one place and I got restless. That's another way the Universe has of tricking us into the experiences we need to fulfill our soul.

I continued hitching and hiking my way around the world, with a year in Alaska, another in India, extended stays in London and Wales. I was jailed in Italy for having a vision/seizure on a public beach — not recommended in any country where you don't speak the language. I survived the sinking of a fishing boat off the island of Kodiak in Alaska, and being thrown overboard off the coast of Calcutta; more jails, more goddesses, more Spirit, a lot more Prune. I was triggering stargates all over the planet, facilitating the end of the karmic day, stuff like that. Of course, I didn't know that's what I was doing. I didn't know anything. Eventually, I settled down long enough to take a wife and two degrees; got a job, taught for awhile, even had a daughter; to her mother's chagrin she seems to have inherited my disease, whatever that is: too much lusting after Spirit, perhaps. It's not a matter of how much is available or how much do you want, but how much are you willing to be responsible for.

And I am learning to suffer the Universe lightly, though it continues to stalk and track me down with a change of consciousness now and again. I like it. But it's not always convenient. And I am still prone to lose large chunks of time — days, weeks, even months I can't account for. It took me almost seven years to work my way around the world that first time. Hardly anyone noticed I was gone, and nobody knew where to.

* * *